KALPANA SHARMA is an independent journalist and author based in Mumbai. In over four decades as a journalist, she has worked with *Himmat Weekly, The Indian Express, Times of India* and *The Hindu,* and was Consulting Editor with *Economic & Political Weekly* and Readers' Editor with *Scroll.in.* She is the author of *Rediscovering Dharavi: Stories from Asia's Largest Slum.*

Advice on Marriage.

TO YOUNG LADIES.

1. Do not marry at all.

2. But if you must avoid the Beauty Men, Flirts, and the Bounders, Tailor's Dummies, and the Football Enthusiasts.

3. Look for a Strong, Tame Man, a Fire-lighter, Coal-getter, Window Cleaner, and Yard Swiller.

4. Don't except too much, most men are lazy, selfish, thoughtless, lying, drunken, clumsy, heavy-footed, rough, unmanly brutes, and need taming.

5. All Bachelors are, and many are worse still.

6. If you want him to be happy, Feed the Brute.

7. The same remark applies to Dogs.

8. You will be wiser not to chance it, it isn't worth the risk.

A SUFFRAGETTE WIFE.

A.F.J.—P.   No. 1327.

Single by Choice
happily unmarried women!

edited by
KALPANA SHARMA

women
UNLIMITED
an associate of
kali for women

Single by Choice:
happy unmarried women!
was first published in India in 2019
by
Women Unlimited
(an associate of Kali for Women)
7/10, First Floor, Sarvapriya Vihar
New Delhi – 110 016

www.womenunlimited.net

ISBN: 978-93-85606-22-9

Cover design: Neelima Rao

Typeset by Manmohan Kumar, Delhi – 110 035
and printed at Raj Press, R–3, Inderpuri, New Delhi – 110 012

Contents

Introduction

Simply single

KALPANA SHARMA

EVENTUALLY, MOST PEOPLE GET MARRIED. EVEN IF THEY DELAY the inevitable, it cannot be put off forever. At least, that is the conventional wisdom. Yet, there are people, men and women, who are not married, have never been married and do not intend to get married. For women, especially, remaining single in a society like ours is unusual, an exception. Who are these women who choose to be different, and embrace their choice of being happily unmarried? We set out to explore this question.

Gloria Steinem, the renowned feminist whose writings have influenced generations of women across the world, once dismissed the institution of marriage as one that destroys relationships. Yet in 2000, at the age of 66, she married David Hale. Several years later, in 2011, in an interview to *The Observer*, Steinem said:

> Remember my age. I didn't know that I had a choice for a long time. I didn't want to get married and have children but I thought it was inevitable, and so I kept saying: not right now. I kept putting it off. After feminism, I suddenly realised: not everyone has to live the same way. Imagine that!

She went on to say that having worked to make marriage more equal, she was glad to have had a chance to take advantage of it.

In India, we are still a very long way from marriages that are equal. As an institution, marriage remains embedded in patriarchy. It is rarely questioned. As women, irrespective of caste, class or creed, we grow up accepting that to be married at some point in life is normal; not to do so is, therefore, abnormal.

When some women decide not to marry, there is an element of choice, but also of happenstance. You didn't meet someone you really wanted to marry. Or you did meet someone you wanted to marry, but he was the wrong man. Or you decided that this thing called marriage was really not your cup of tea, and that you were better off on your own. The reasons vary from person to person, but there is one constant factor that emerges: questions about the institution of marriage as it currently exists in India.

From the time you hit your teens, you are expected by family, society and your peers, to 'find someone'. In more conservative communities, your family looks for that 'someone' for you. If you are urban, middle-class, educated and perhaps have parents who are professionals, you might be permitted to look for that person yourself, although your choice will be vetted by them and your larger family.

By the time you're in your twenties, most other women around you will be married or on the verge of it. Even if you are not, your family will not stop the search for a potential husband. Photographs are sent, horoscopes exchanged, caste matched, class status checked out, and a 'meeting' takes place. If all this clicks into place, the marriage is firmed up.

If you survive your twenties and enter your thirties without getting married, you are most likely to be left alone by your family. They look to divine intervention to help you find a suitable boy. If that doesn't work, they probably comfort themselves with the thought that they will have someone to care for them in their old age.

Is this beginning to change? As more women enter professions that earlier were closed to them, become economically independent, confident of their ability to negotiate life without a man around, are they consciously deciding not to get married? This does not mean that they are averse to romantic relationships—with men or women. It is just that they are unconvinced that getting married brings anything new into their already full lives; they have no urge to hunt for an appropriate and acceptable partner. If someone comes along who fits the bill, perhaps marriage can be considered, otherwise, remaining single is becoming an acceptable way to live.

We thought it might be interesting to explore why some Indian women consciously decide to remain single. While women of an earlier generation probably remained so without actually planning it, today we are seeing more urban, middle class, educated Indian women deciding to either delay marriage, or not marry at all.

This anthology consists of essays by women in different age groups—60 years and up, between 40 and 50 years, and 40 and younger. The contributors are writers, journalists, a lawyer, a sociologist, a scientist, an editor, and a pioneer in promoting Indian hand-woven textiles and handicrafts. Together, they represent many different experiences and perspectives. Although all the essays are personal histories, recounted with honesty and humour, there are several common threads that run through them.

Although the title of this collection is *Single by Choice*, many of the writers point out that it was not a simple matter of choice alone. Did any of us single women really decide that we wanted to be so? Some contributors say that it was a conscious decision; others admit that the choice came much later. In the words of Laila Tyabji,

> I didn't actually ever take a decision that I wouldn't get married. For people of my generation, even those educated on western lines in liberal non-convent schools, it seemed the obvious finale

to growing up. We all were set on going to college and planned to work for a while afterwards, but marriage and a family was always the final piece of the picture.

Laila's observations reflect what many older women, including myself, went through. We did not consciously set out to remain unmarried for the rest of our lives, but there came a point when we did make that choice, and having made it, we are convinced that it was the right decision for us.

Younger women, however, are already convinced that marriage is not the 'obvious finale'. They are raising questions about the institution of marriage. Not just arranged marriages, against which women of an older generation also rebelled, but marriage itself. Sharanya Gopinathan, our youngest contributor, admits that for many like her, rebelling against marriage was restricted to the matter of choice. It did not, she writes, 'explore breaking out of the inherently restrictive, regressive, and casteist structure of marriage itself'. Yet, today, there are women like her who are questioning this structure as it exists in India.

Others are not against getting married, but find the current configuration of the marital status dysfunctional for women who are making independent financial decisions and holding their own in a variety of professions. If the dominant norms that dictate a woman's status within the institution of marriage are not acceptable to women of this generation, what is their notion of an ideal marriage? Rhea Saran, also from among the younger writers, says that in her view marriage,

> ... is about partnership, in the truest sense of the word, and about both partners having choices. It's about a fluid sort of equality that swings one way or the other at different points of time, and in different situations and aspects of life. It's about there being a balance.

Can such a balance be achieved without upturning patriarchy? Rhea remains hopeful that one day it could happen. So does Aditi Bishnoi, who suggests that 'if there was ever a time to get married on one's terms, it is now; and if there was ever a time to choose to remain single, it is now.' Thus, even if some younger women are not drifting into marriage automatically, they are questioning the terms of engagement and expecting them to be drastically reformed. Till then, they are consciously choosing to step away from marriage.

Although both older and younger women write about the many joys of remaining single, happiness and contentment do not come easily or automatically to all of them. The well-known Tamil Dalit writer, Bama, in her searing essay, writes about the challenges she faced not just as a single woman, but as an unmarried Dalit woman. Finding a place to live was virtually impossible, she writes. 'In that rural atmosphere, for those around me I was an object of unending curiosity, as if I were a totally different creature!' She had no one to help her when she was ill and people, including other women, were only too ready to cast aspersions on her character *because* she was unmarried. Bama's story is a necessary reality check. It reminds us that even for accomplished and economically independent women, caste remains an important and unchanging marker.

Many of those who have written mention a question they are often asked, 'What will you do when you get old?' Yet, that is a question that applies to everyone, married or single. Those who are married now, might find themselves single at some point in their lives. Even if they have children, they cannot take for granted that they will be around to look after them. So, how is that any different from those who never married? I would argue that the latter may actually make plans because they cannot assume that someone will be there to look after them.

There are also decisions about life, including marriage, that are made within the political milieu in which we grow up. Both Sujata Patel, whose Gandhian parents were deeply involved in the freedom movement, and Vineeta Bal who, apart from being a scientist, has also been engaged in feminist struggles, write about the role that this larger politics played in their decisions to remain single.

It is possible that certain professions exert a greater pressure on women to remain unmarried. Vineeta Bal, for instance, quotes data from a survey on the marital status of scientists that found that '13 per cent of women trained as scientists had never married. In contrast, only two per cent of the men interviewed were single.' Demanding professions place an additional burden on women, especially if they want to get ahead.

Sometimes, the particular community to which you belong helps; conversely, it could also be the reason why you face more pressure. As Parsis, Freny Manecksha and Sherna Gandhy were not pressed by their families to agree to arranged marriages, but they had to contend with the narrative of a shrinking population within their community, because women were either staying single, or marrying later and not having children, or marrying out of the community.

In this context, Freny asks questions that apply to all cultures:

Why is it (marriage) seen as 'inevitable' for a woman, especially in our cultures? Is our role as women confined to being home-maker and baby producer? Why are these the only 'markers of adulthood', with celebrations centred on events like a wedding anniversary, the birth of children and later still, the children's weddings? What is this insistence on seeing women as gaining in responsibility and respect only through marriage? Why are women, who refuse to conform, called old maids or frustrated spinsters, or as people who have not quite made the grade?

The 'old maids' in this book are far from frustrated and have certainly made the grade!

While all the essays focus on personal choice, Freny and Aheli Moitra have included the experiences of other single women they met, or with whom they have worked. Aheli has chosen to work as a journalist in Nagaland. Her stories about how she has navigated her life as an 'outsider', and that, too, as a single woman in Nagaland, are immensely entertaining. Equally fascinating is her account about the challenges Naga women face if they remain single in a society where women's roles are defined within specific tribal cultures. She writes,

> Single women in the Naga hills have no right to inheritance of ancestral property…They have marginal voices in family or clan and village meetings. Without a husband or child to claim social legitimacy, the choice to remain single here is harder still. Yet the choice is becoming easier to make for women who want to, or can, study, work, and earn enough to buy their own property.

Even in a state like Maharashtra, with a long tradition of women's emancipation, a woman remaining unmarried is an exception, especially in rural areas. Freny writes about one such woman who appears to be as happily unmarried as is Freny. Laila Tyabji also describes women in Rajasthan and Kashmir with whom she works, who have excelled as craftswomen, and have also remained single within their deeply conservative milieu. There must be hundreds more such stories that can be excavated and recorded, but we will leave that for another book!

What emerges from all the essays is the willingness of these women to carve out a unique and different pathway for their lives. I liked the way Sharda Ugra, a pioneering woman sports journalist, describes women like herself and the rest of us:

> I think of India's single women across generations as being re-decorators, reshapers, renovators of a sort. Of the rooms and

boxes in which not only women, even men, people at large, have always been told where and how they must live.

Breaking out of boxes. That is indeed an appropriate way to describe what many single women are doing in India.

———————

Putting together this anthology has not been easy. Many women agreed to write but found they were unable to do so. It is quite understandable that not everyone wants to reveal their personal lives. A subject like this necessarily requires something about ourselves to be revealed, and also involves exposing our families and friends. It is our loss that many of the brilliant women who could have written, did not.

Those who have, are exceptionally courageous in allowing us to enter their lives, to be introduced to their families, and to learn about their personal journeys that ultimately led to a state of singleness. They also narrate the fun and drama along the way, of the failed attempts to set them up, of the persistent questions people ask because they just cannot accept that a single woman can be happy and content. Laila Tyabji says she fantasised about a T-shirt with the words, 'I've had 15 proposals. I am single by choice!'

A striking feature in practically all the accounts is the presence of supportive parents who let their daughters decide what they wanted to do and be. That is an essential prerequisite, and certainly far from being the norm. The pressure that parents face to get their daughters 'settled' is immense. Against this, for them to accept that their daughter knows what she wants and should be trusted to follow her own star, is rare. We are the lucky ones.

As important as supportive parents is the fact that all the women who have written have a profession, one that is engaging and satisfying. Most of us are economically independent and therefore in a position to decide what we want to do with our lives. We can make choices, and are in a position to defend them. Furthermore, a rewarding professional life not only gives us the social capital that independent women need, but also an alternative community, comprising friends and colleagues, that is supportive and inclusive.

There are many echoes of my own story in the essays that follow, such as supportive parents—in my case, one parent. My father became a widower at 40, with three young children, and chose not to remarry. He allowed the three of us to grow up without too much pressure to conform, although I am sure he secretly hoped that we wouldn't turn out to be too outlandish! Fortunately for him, we did not, although we are all non-conformists. Each of us made our own choices—of profession, about when and whether to marry, and if the latter, then whom to marry. This was inevitable, given that we were the children of a father who also chose his own bride, against the wishes of both families.

I was once on the cusp of marriage, at the age of 27. Like other women my age, I presumed that I had to get married some day and so, why not now, to the man who had proposed to me. I dipped my toe into the marriage pool and quickly withdrew. I was called a 'coward'; told that I had to have the courage to 'take the plunge'; that marriage was a gamble anyway. Well, I decided I am not the gambling type. In hindsight, it was a wise decision, both for me and for my intended. If I had indeed plunged into that pool it would have been something of a disaster. Of this, I am now certain.

I think, again with hindsight, that the toe-dipping exercise was possibly the beginning of my awakening to the fact that there is life outside marriage. Not consciously at first, but over time. The process of questioning that made me withdraw from marriage led me to ask many more questions about the place of women in our society, about the reasons for inequality and injustice, about the kind of world I wanted to see. It was the gateway that directed me towards what I am today—a feminist, a peacenik, an environmentalist—who believes that you cannot build a just world if half its people, women, are given secondary status; who is convinced that we have to find ways to avert war and violence; and who seeks ways to build an environmentally sustainable society, where we conserve what cannot be replaced and consume only what we need.

I also believe, as several women in this book have articulated, that 'family' does not mean only those related by blood. Sujata Patel points out that she realised how 'by creating a friendship network that bonded over public concerns', her parents and their friends 'were also creating an alternate family/kin group, based on non-blood relationships'. We can create such families of choice. They are as nurturing and caring, sometimes even more so, than those we are born into, or marry into. Perhaps because, as singles, we cannot take such relationships for granted, we make a greater effort to cherish and sustain such 'families'. I have certainly benefitted from these alternative support structures, made up of people of different ages, varying professions, but with a basic commonality in terms of shared values.

On a lighter note, Sharda mentions a 2011 book, *Savvy Auntie: The Ultimate Guide for Cool Aunts, Great-Aunts, Godmothers, and All Women Who Love Kids* by Melanie Notkin. Apparently, this book came up with the acronym, PANK (Professional Aunt No Kids). I have absolutely no objection to being a PANK! As Asmita Basu says, many of us singletons are irreplaceable and much-loved aunts. I love being an aunty, and am known to spoil all the children who decide to bestow that title on me, including the two kids who live next door. Variously called 'maushi', 'masi', 'atya' or plain old aunty, I revel in their love, and am glad I don't have to deal with their tantrums!

This book is not a sociological survey; it is a reflection. It notes the existence of singleness, as in never-married. It outlines, through the experiences of the twelve women contributors representing a range of experience, cutting across several generations, the questions that women like them are asking: about Indian society and its attitude towards women; about the institution of marriage; about patriarchy; about independence and equality.

These questions are relevant, irrespective of marital status or gender. We hope that they provoke more debate and discussion on these and related subjects. Perhaps, one day, we will begin to see a transformation of that stubbornly unchanging concept: the Great Indian Marriage.

Stomping on the cookie-cutter

SHARDA UGRA

AS MUCH AS THE FACT HOVERS BETWEEN CORNY AND CLICHÉD, this piece cannot be written without cricket. Cricketers, actually. They are part of my life story as a singleton/bachelor girl/spinster. The story is not about how I found one or two or three cricketers compellingly attractive and *how they turned out to be heels and broke my heart and that is why I am single...* Not even close.

It is more about how cricket and cricketers first made me process the idea of singlehood, and then understand how the outside world deals with it. When Kalpana asked me to write about being single (*what's the word here—deliberately? purposefully? purposely? stubbornly?*) and I began to work through memories, cricket and cricketers kept showing up.

I remember precisely the first—and only—time my father asked me the 'What Are You Planning To Do With Your Life?' question—code for *shaadi* talk. It was November 26, 1995, just around noon. I'd just turned 27, my Dad was driving us somewhere for Sunday lunch. There is a reason I remember the date and time but not where we were going. Cricket commentary was on on the radio—India were playing New Zealand in a one-day match in Nagpur, and this madcap Kiwi batsman had pulverised our bowling. On Mumbai's Eastern Express Highway, just after Nathan Astle completes his debut ODI century, my Dad throws a hand grenade onto the back seat.

It took a while to explode because my reply was about applying for a journalism fellowship and travelling for a bit. After which the M word detonated good and proper. With Astle just having completed his century, India being well and truly stuffed, the coolest parents in the world (and they remain so) led me into an ambush. Naturally, everything that followed the question meant that Astle's hundred was seared onto my mind forever. The matter did sort itself out within a few months (more on that later) but the sheer incongruity of staying optionally single, unmarried, unhitched was noted.

More than ten years on—a decade-plus of personal and professional singleton adventures—it was only when a cricket friend came home for lunch did I first get an idea of what my life looked like to the outside world. My friend, standing in the middle of my living room in Delhi, asks, 'Did you do all this'? He is waving his hands around at sofas, cushions, a carpet, a bookcase, paintings, photos on the wall, a TV set in a corner. The table was set for lunch, mats et al, and my friend was half-baffled, half-bemused as he acknowledged curtains, crockery, photos, music, books. Yes, of course, I'd done all *this*. '*Who else?*'

I'd known my friend for almost as long as I'd been a sports journalist. Perceptive, compassionate, fun. I understood instantly where his question came from: the box in which single Indian women were usually housed. Where, while growing up, I'd seen singlehood translate itself in the movies, books, television, across social whisper. It presented the woman as an entity unfulfilled, incomplete and, leading from there, eventually unhappy. Whose surroundings, it was imagined—and no doubt still is—would be dark, forlorn, gloomy, unkempt and, of course, only half of what a home should be. My cricketer-pal had got used to the idea of my singleness while working or travelling; at lunch that afternoon, he saw what it looked like at the back end. What provoked this question perhaps, was its sheer normalcy.

The notion of singlehood as a possibly desired way of life came to me from an unusual source—my mother. As I came into adulthood, I discovered that my mother's love for the family and her generous sociability were tied in with a mind of her own, an empathetic, democratic spirit and untempered adventure-seeking fearlessness. She once told me that had she not been an obedient daughter to our Nani, she would never have married. She would have been happy, she thought, to spend her life in books, reading, writing and looking after the family around her in hometown Narsinghpur, Madhya Pradesh.

This was not what mothers usually told their daughters, but it stayed with me. That in the late-1950s, as a young woman, she had contemplated singlehood and was not self-conscious about sharing this. Plus the fact that if not for her adoration of, and responsibility towards, her mother, she would have been unafraid to go down that path, regardless of the boxes that women in the 1960s were being stuffed into to keep them in line. Before marrying my father in 1964, when she was 22, she had thought through an alternative life for herself. This was in an age when single women from their late 20s onwards were usually slotted as either tragic or demonic; either wilting willows waiting to be rescued into marriage by an elderly widower, or 'angry' 'frustrated', vampish sisters-in-law to their brothers' wives, the kind of characters still being trotted out on daily soaps. If my mother had had her way, she had been willing to contest and aim to reinvent this image. Wow. In the Mommy-DNA-lottery, I realised I'd struck the jackpot.

In hindsight, I accepted that the Nathan Astle conversation was only my parents doing their desi parental duty. In fact, when I was around 16, my pragmatic mother had given me a choice. Did I want my father and her to look for a husband for me or would I find some fellow myself? If the former, she said, she would go about ensuring that I was trained into being a good wife. Cooking, housekeeping, consideration for others, and knowing when to compromise for the sake of the larger collective, aka Family. If I chose the latter route, she let it be known that I could not return weeping to my parents, aged 35, asking them to please, please find me a suitable groom. The curious social engineering of arranged marriages had always appeared severely imbalanced to me; the heavy lifting was almost always supposed to be done by the women. My mother wasn't surprised by my answer—*please don't take the trouble, I'll manage.*

I'd thought the business had been taken care of earlier, which is why Nathan and I were so blindsided that afternoon. Yet, looking at it from my parents' point of view, they had no choice but to check on my marriage prospects again: my father, always patient and supportive of my life and career choices, would be retiring in a year and heading back to Allahabad where he came from. I had taken a loan off them for a 482 sq ft apartment in Nerul, Navi Mumbai, and in the mid-1990s, it was not *de rigueur* for single, middle-class women to live by themselves, even if they owned the damn flat. The sprawling, loving arms of our family would be asking my parents the question about their daughter's 'future', and no matter my modern education and its freedoms, some medieval questions had to be raised. And raised again.

My response was to cut off the just-meet-the-boy routine at its first, lone appearance. There were phone conversations with concerned relatives, and even a few friends, about my stubborn refusal to go down that path. For about a month, maybe less, I remember reacting to the situation, 'like a man': I would come home late from office and not talk. Arranged marriage to me, I told 'well-wishers', was like 'eating through my nose'. If things didn't work out in the singles-trying-to-double-up market, I thought I was ready to remain un'settled'. That position ignored the societal pressures that my parents would be put under, and also paid no heed to the accepted wisdom of a woman's yearning for motherhood, or that other unanswerable: 'Who will look after you in your old age?'

As urban societies evolve, throwing up new fissures in established relationships and giving rise to wellsprings of hidden alliances, that last question, we realise, could apply to everyone. Man, woman, single, hitched. More than ever the answer to *who will look after you in your old age* remains a 50-50 call. A 2011 Census statistic which revealed that there were 71 million single women in India, a 39 per cent increase from the turn of the new millennium, had me whooping with triumph, before I looked deeper. Even if you deduct the number of widowed, divorced or separated, the number of women who have never married, for whatever reason, is still formidable: 13.2 million in rural India and 12.3 million in urban India, a grand total of 25.2 million. To arrive at a figure of the urban, economically independent single women whose stories are told in this book, we must slice and dice more. The 2011 Census found that the number of urban single women had gone up from 17.1 million in 2001 to 27 million in 2011. Of those 27 million, even if we assume that only 10 per cent are single by wild, wilful choice, it's still 2.7 million women, the populations of Lithuania, Jamaica and Qatar. We are certainly not alone.

My mother was not the first woman I would know of who had thought about a life without children. As time passed, more than one friend would tell me about the hard grind that motherhood and parenthood were. About the boldness of their aspirations being steadily bleached into a pastel of family expectations and sometimes incomplete contentment. Yet, very little of this reaches single women in their 20s or 30s. At that age all we are told about is the human instinct for mateship and then companionship ('It's not about the sex, sometimes you just need someone to cuddle in the morning,' this too from a cricketer-pal) or the countdown of the female body clock and the terror of 'alone'. Cinema and popular culture appear to be driven by this inalienable, unshakeable truth with its Hollywood horror trope—you will die alone. Technically speaking, everyone dies alone, in their bodies and in their heads. The trick is to build a community while we're on our way there.

What I could not understand was why no distinction was made between aching loneliness—which can swallow people whole even in large family groups—and the freedom of solitary calm. Why was it seen as too dangerous for women to even be offered a glimpse of the solitary (outside celibate nunhood, that is) before hardwiring us through adolescence into being carers and nurturers responsible for the propagation of the family/ clan/ human race? Bringing up children never became a yearning for me, but this was not something you openly declared, as somehow it made you less of a woman. Childlessness came second on the list of misdemeanours for an Indian woman—after unmarried, that is. (New on the list in this twisted era of no-can-dos are *love jihad* or caste-proofed marriages.) Society—Indian, western, eastern—has only one cookie-cutter that women must fit themselves into. All the rest on offer to young adolescent women is merely a series of horror stories. How do you free yourself of this? How do you find yourself?

———————————

I accept that I am fortunate and privileged to be able to do what I want to do—stomp on the cookie-cutter, walk out of the bakery itself and pitch my tent elsewhere. What I discovered is that there is a lot of free space in Elsewhere. When I moved into my first self-owned apartment in Navi Mumbai, aged 28, I didn't feel I was being radical or brave or striking one for womanhood. I was merely creating a foothold in the city I was born in, worked in and loved. My parents braced themselves for having me turn up again, defeated by the Alone Monster, seeking rescue by the Companion. It was only a matter of time. I remember my father's time limit as being six months tops (he denies having any such window, small or big) and my mother's, 18 months (she has no such memory either).

Only after their first visits did they decide to stop fretting about my anticipated struggles against singlehood. The house was in order, tidy, looked after, running. It was a tiny ground floor 1BHK overlooking a small garden, determined as I was, like all Bombaywallas, to seek 'tree views'. When people walking past its balcony peeked in, they often found a woman reading, watching TV, or eating while doing either. My mother had armed me suitably; she filled a diary full of recipes and wrote a suggested schedule to keep my fridge full, my kitchen running, and my stomach sated. Neighbours were gently curious, but neither interfering nor judgemental. I invited friends over for weekend sleepovers and Sunday lunches.

Every morning, my train journey to work (when on time, I could always, every single day, grab a second class window seat facing the breeze) would take me over the vast, serene

Vashi creek headlong into the noise and energy of the-then Bombay. At night on my return home, I could see and hear the crowd and the noise of the great city fall away behind the moving train. I could have lived there forever. I had friends and family all over Bombay, we would meet, work, celebrate, and then, whatever the duration of the journey, the trains would take me back to my castle. Hostel life, both as student and working woman, was perfect training for self-reliance and being part of a community of friends who relied on each other. To have my own patch in Bombay was validation and affirmation of how I wanted to live. In the three decades that have passed since, I have changed jobs and cities twice, travelled, remained in touch with a vast circle of friends and family—and dealt with having contracted multiple sclerosis. Due to which I was once utterly miserable about having to admit myself to hospital (only because I stupidly didn't reach out and ask any of my many friends to accompany me) but still enjoyed the utter, unfettered freedom of being single.

After the MS began to play itself out, my parents moved in with me, and that is how we live now, settling into patterns and habits. My father has got drawn into home renovations for two residences, one in Navi Mumbai and the other in Noida. I do not argue with my mother's methods in the running of the house and kitchen. Independence married inter-dependence, and it works fine. If I have to identify when I became more or less sure about not wanting to 'settle' for the sake of 'settling', it was when I moved into my tiny flat in Navi Mumbai. It may sound like the heresy of the arrogant, but that place and that time gave me the chance to ask a question of Marriage itself—what is it you offer me in exchange for turning away from this life?

———————

In my profession as a sports journalist, being a woman was the first marker of oddness. There weren't any such around when I began in 1989; our numbers began to grow slowly in the early 1990s, and for the better part of the decade, trying to gain acceptance as a working professional amongst athletes and administrators was a priority. As time passed, being single may have been noted by the industry, but only a very small slice commented on my singleness. For the majority, maybe I was just a deviant to begin with, anyway, so singlehood was only to be expected.

Once, in my 20s, a senior journalist asked me if I was 'interested' in starting a conversation about marriage with an 'interested' fellow pro, whose name I was not told. I politely declined. Across the years, another media friend asked me repeatedly about why I was still single. I would be linked to single men known to us, and I dutifully laughed at the many jokes that were cracked. Questions often floated through from a variety of sources: 'You haven't met anyone?' 'Haven't you met *anyyyyvann* you like?' 'Ohh, you don't like boys?' 'Do you like (involuntary, pale-faced, shudder) *girls*?'

Facts first. I *lurve* boys, more accurately, men. (And yo, you go, girls who like girls.) Men who don't take themselves too seriously can make you laugh; the knee-knocking ones who make my knees knock; the politically-incorrect good souls (some, not all) over the politically-correct deep thinkers who (some not all) it is later proved, eventually want the women of their dreams to be dreamy chapatti makers. But—and it's an epic all caps BUT—I don't feel fervently compelled to be hooked-up, coupled or married to them. Nothing against the institution, may it long prosper and make millions deliriously happy, but as I've grown older, I realise it's not an institution I want to sign myself into.

When compared to the western world, I've always found India to be a far easier place to grow old in, single. The questions stop post-35ish and you are then allowed to just be—solo, slightly loco, we who may or may not become 'burdens' on familial branches, and the less they get in your way, the better. Out in the developed world, the pressure of a Friday night date or any kind of date any time, or a 'partner' as the measure of an individual's social success seems like a relentless source of anxiety. In a way, single women are like solo travellers and the world, like the travel industry as it once seemed, finds them hard to handle or even logistically cope with. This hit home when I lived in Australia for a couple of months while on a fellowship, in 2013. Want to go to the Great Barrier Reef for a mad single day trip? Pairs only. Want to travel to Uluru and need a single room? Not possible. Pay for two, or travel with someone.

To be honest, having travelled extensively on work, I now prefer travelling in company, with plans, thoughts, experiences, stresses and costs shared. From among my oldest, closest friends whom I went to college with, I am the only singleton. We've known each other for more than thirty-four years and I know I have lucked out with them. They are my posse, my long-distance entourage, the keepers of secrets, their non-judgementalism consistent, their cheerleading reality-checked, their spouses still locked out of our now-infrequent but still sacred pyjama parties, just like when we were 16. We joke about racing our wheelchairs in retirement homes, with them ticking me off for inappropriately eyeing disreputable, lost-cause 85 year-old-men. Everyone needs them, friends who knew you before you put on your armour and mask and headed into the working world. Which is where single women collect fellow travellers and comrades and add to their citadel; I have found them in hostels, in offices, during work travels, while moving cities. We connect and re-connect, and now that the majority are into our 40s and 50s, out of shape, beat-up, menopausal, cranky, we talk about how we will handle life slowing down, sharing advice and tips. In our heads, we are no older than somewhere between 16 and 26.

The benefits of being married, I have joked, is having bed-tea served to you on some mornings. The benefit of being single, I tell those who still ask is, 'See, I spared two families from being miserable.' The happily married, though, make me joyful. As a serial attender of family-and-friend-weddings, I fully appreciate that it is they who maintain the order and demographic balance of the world, a sizeable number of them doing the needful already. I welcome the arrival of children and enjoy watching them grow into entertaining, argumentative versions of the people I have known and love. A 2011 book, *Savvy Auntie: The Ultimate Guide for Cool Aunts, Great-Aunts, Godmothers, and All Women Who Love Kids* by Melanie Notkin gave the world an acronym: PANK (Professional Aunt No Kids). I find it a bit limited, not fully describing the splendour and freedom of singledom.

In any case, I think the adjectives sometimes used around us, a little churlishly, are 'irresponsible' 'selfish' and 'scared.' Whatever. I humbly suggest that our contributions to society are slightly more-wide ranging—answering the 2 a.m. phone call; discussing world issues and gossip; offering shoulders to cry on; standing in as nth hour baby-minders or housekeepers or cat feeders. We are the aunts (and uncles) who hand out goodies to nephews and nieces and kids of friends, only to find 'return gifts' falling into our laps years later. Like the time in London when, reaching for my wallet in a hip Soho restaurant, my niece sitting across me gave me the gold-standard millennial eye roll and said, languidly dismissive, 'Masi, please...'

I think of India's single women across generations as being redecorators, reshapers, renovators, of a sort. Of the rooms and boxes in which not only women, but even men, people at large, have always been told where and how they must live. If my friend's question about home décor startled me into imagining my life from the outside, another niece's response (my last count of nephews and nieces via cousins hit 26) showed me what a new generation saw. My niece was buzzed, she said, to see my name on a name-plate outside my flat. She found the sight cool in its humdrumness, like what she was used to seeing—her father or her friends' fathers' names outside their offices and homes. Then, one day, her aunt's name outside hers. Just like that.

Being single is not being solitary

LAILA TYABJI

WANDERING AROUND INDIA AS I DO, THE FIRST QUESTION I am asked is how many children I have. Whether the question is posed in a village gathering, a railway carriage, a college cafeteria, or a conference, nobody questions for a minute that a respectable-looking 71 year old MUST be married, and therefore a mother. When I reveal that I am single, and always have been, the reactions are varied—compassion, astonishment, blank disbelief and, occasionally, envy.

Some years ago, a young journalist came to see me for a story on my work. As she concluded the interview, she said, 'Ma'am, I know you said no personal questions, but I just wanted to tell you how much I admire you.' She was under the illusion that I had selflessly sacrificed marriage and children for a life devoted to Dastkar and craftspeople. When I laughingly pointed out that being single didn't mean being sad or solitary; or, for that matter, celibate, she seemed shocked out of her wits and rapidly exited, dropping her pad and leaving her pencil behind. The vision of Saint Laila, vestal virgin in the cause of craft, had gone up in smoke.

I didn't actually ever take a decision that I wouldn't get married. For people of my generation, even those educated on western lines in liberal non-convent schools, it seemed the obvious finale to growing up. We were all set on going to college and planned to work for a while afterwards, but marriage and a family was always the final piece of the picture. Practically the end of the story. The books we read, whether Jane Austen or Mills & Boon, all had the same trajectory.

For me, growing up with three brothers plus many male cousins and their friends, the opposite sex were neither the heroes nor the heartthrobs my classmates fantasised about. I was too much at ease to be easily enamoured. It was disconcerting, though, to discover that while teenage girls spent inordinate amounts of their time talking about boys, how little we seemed to figure in theirs! And a surprise that their schoolboy jokes about sex seemed to mean something quite different from our own roseate visions of romantic 'love'!

Leaving school in 1962, only one of my classmates had a clear career plan—she wanted to be a doctor. We were 15 or 16, and most of us were pretty hazy about the options. I remember my friends vacillating between advertising, being teachers, UN translators, or even air hostesses (in those days of foreign exchange shortage, it was the only way to go abroad!). But at the end of this brief bout of independence was always a husband. Dim, undefined, but definitely the dominant presence.... The more daring said, 'I'll never have an arranged marriage' or, even more boldly, 'Race and religion no bar.' but NO ONE (even those who seemed to prefer the company of girls) said, 'I am not going to get married.' This despite the shining example of our Headmistress, Miss Grace Linnell, who'd come out to India after World War 1, lived with her best friend, and was instrumental in teaching generations of Indian girls, first in Hyderabad and then at Welham, how to think for themselves; to be fearless, independent, and questioning.

Like my peers, I, too, took marriage as something that would happen eventually: spontaneously, inevitably, and without much effort on my part. Since I had neither social nor economic pressures egging me on, I put the matter on the back burner. Meanwhile, I spent a happy time at art school in Baroda and another two years in Japan, and then, with another year-long interval in Japan, life as a free-lance designer in my barsati in Defence Colony. Shy and painfully conscious of being the plain Jane daughter of two very good-looking parents, I was relieved to find that I wasn't totally unattractive to men! Artists had their attractions, but I didn't want to marry any of them. I knew that I didn't want to be a diplomat's wife either, like my mother. Nor, despite succumbing briefly to the beguiling charms of first an Englishman, and then a young Frenchman, did I want to marry and live abroad, a perpetual foreigner. Moreover, life on my own terms seemed increasingly delightful and, gradually, the compromises and adjustments of marriage seemed more and more claustrophobic. My idea of bliss became 'a lover who lived down the lane'.

Kalpana Sharma has written about 'the rocky terrain that every Indian woman must traverse as she approaches the inevitability of marriage'. Mercifully I never encountered any rocks. My parents, possibly recognising my maverick views on the matter, never took it for granted that I would or should marry. I don't know if they had anguished midnight conclaves on the subject, but they seemed remarkably relaxed, concentrating their efforts on my eldest brother, born to be a family man but diffident about achieving it.

Nor was there pressure or social opprobrium from the extended family. Luckily, I had some formidable aunts who had led the way. One, Raihana Tyabji, was a Sufi mystic who was part of Gandhiji's inner group. She remained single all her life, living in an ashram, singing Mira bhajans in her beautiful voice, and writing a book, *Heart of a Gopi*, in which she described her experiences as a Krishna devotee. I would visit her with my parents on our trips to Delhi, and loved the way she combined a matter-of-fact but intense spirituality with a passion for chocolates and detective novels.

Closer to us, and a trailblazing icon for any adolescent, was my father's younger sister, Kamila. According to family legend, despite also being ferociously intelligent, Kamila's flirtatious ways had been a great worry to her parents in her teens. She went off to Oxford and then joined the Bar, the first Indian Muslim woman to do so. She then settled in London to practise law, becoming the first woman ever to plead a case in the Privy Council. Much courted by many, including a Sinhalese prime minister, she remained resolutely single, with a lifelong attachment to an eccentric Sri Lankan with whom she and a group of equally unconventional friends—artists, actors, and other professionals—shared a home for over three decades. She only left London and 'The Family', as they called themselves, in the mid-1960s, to join Jayaprakash Narayan's Sarvodaya Movement in Bihar, after the great Famine. Finding him inspirational but the movement chaotic and muddled, she moved to Bombay to start the Women's India Trust (WIT), getting the famous underworld Don, Haji Mastaan, to give her a donation for sewing machines. He apparently admired the way she drove her sky-blue Rover into the narrow slum lanes and chawls of the city, looking for needy housebound women to train. Kamila Phupu loved the company of men, but felt women were far more sensible, down-to-earth, and competent!

Apparently, my mother (whose best friend she'd been, growing up) predicted from my infancy that, 'Laila is going to be another Kamila'. Certainly, my first conscious view of this glamorous aunt in London, when I was 10, made me her lifelong fan. Six-foot-eight, dressed always in flamboyant saris and jewellery, witty and successful (Sean Connery was one of her clients), a wonderful speaker, but also a superb cook and seamstress, casually writing a landmark book on Muslim law in her spare time, she seemed such a fun role model. Although I never had her self-confidence and brilliance, the exuberant assurance with which she lived her unconventional life certainly inspired my choices. Even in her mid-80s, she would lie in her ornately carved white bed, early morning, and scan the financial pages of the *Times of India*, then ring up her broker and play the stock market with extraordinary acumen; WIT and the women it supported survived through the success of her investments.

So, were there moments of insecurity and loneliness? My early 30s, with my mother no longer there as a supportive buffer, all the desirable seeming men married, and all my friends absorbed in parenthood, had their spasms of self doubt. Was I always going to be the singleton, the odd one out? The one who drove home alone on my motorbike, while others got into cars with their husbands? The one with no baby stories or mother-in-law jokes? This sounds shamefully feeble, but I think it would have been much more tedious if no one had ever wanted to marry me! The confidence of having been wanted tided me over the trying times dealing with curious impertinent queries of, 'So when is it your turn?' or 'How come you haven't married…?' or even more crassly, 'It's not that you're bad looking…' The implication always was that anyone who could marry, would. It's a rare married woman, however unhappy herself, who can believe a single woman doesn't pine to be married. I sometimes fantasised about a T shirt emblazoned with the message—'I've had 15 proposals. I am single by choice!'

Meanwhile, looking at relationships all around me, and even my parents' long, supportive and happy marriage, it seemed that marriage was inevitably a compromise, with the give and take disproportionately weighted in favour of the male. It was men's jobs that decided where couples would settle, what share they would take in household chores and childcare, whether their wives could work, travel and have independent lives. Adding to everything was the conflict between my predilection for brilliant, creative, complicated types, and my equally strong desire to be my own person!

The men I fancied were wonderful, stimulating company, but were also pretty demanding: clearly not ideal marriage material. The thought of living with them forever gave me pause! Once the intense give and take of early courtship was over, it was a shock that even the most unconventional of Indian men had in mind relationships that were very conventional. I found jealousy and possessiveness unattractive rather than flattering. Being naturally monogamous by nature I had no desire to be unfaithful, but I did want the freedom I had of picking up my jhola and travelling the world, of crafting the multicoloured jigsaw of my life as I chose. I didn't want to 'follow' my man, I wanted us hand-in-hand; and the opportunity to occasionally lead! At the same time I didn't want a doormat as a husband. There was the paradox. Liberated though I was, I still needed my husband to be my intellectual equal if not my superior. The social conditioning of the time made it difficult to change established mindsets.

My father adored and admired my mother, often citing her as the perfect woman. He loved that she painted so well, had such sparkling wit, intelligence and subtle aesthetic, ran a beautiful home, was an admired hostess and ambassador's wife. He trusted her implicitly, and happily handed over the family finances to her care. (She gave him Rs. 100 as pocket money!) But he took it for granted that she would follow where his career took him and make his ambitions her own. Someone for whom family and friends were the centre of her existence, she moved twenty-three times in their married life. In those early years of the Indian Foreign Service, she was separated for most of the year from her children. Disliking the formal, artificial minuet of diplomatic life, she nevertheless ran an embassy effortlessly, mugged up on wines and European etiquette, learnt French, Farsi and Indonesian; on occasion cooking a sit-down five-course state dinner for thirty-five, singlehandedly, at short notice (the cook and his assistant had overdosed on the brandy!). Her one concern was that the hand-kissing German dignitaries would smell garlic on her fingers. But it was only after my father retired to Hyderabad that Amma was able to do what she'd always wanted—design textiles and crafts and work with poor women.

Much later, in the lonely years after her early death, Abba admitted that he had selfishly taken advantage of her unconditional love. He told me, 'I didn't take your mother for granted, but I did take it for granted that she was there primarily for me.' It was this realisation that made him bend backwards, even in extreme old age, not to impose his needs on my life. Meanwhile, my mother's brother, much loved and indulged, a high-flying future air marshal, laughingly admitted that he thought himself very liberal in allowing his wife to take up work assignments 'as long as she is home when I return from office'. My aunt quite happily accepted this as a loveable proof of his affection!

Even though educated, well read, and coming from progressive westernised families, my mother, aunts, and their friends and contemporaries considered themselves lucky to have companionable, appreciative, caring marriages. Surrendering their own independence and aspirations seemed a more than acceptable return. Marriage was their career of choice, a mindset that continued well into the next generation.

As late as the 1960s, my views on marriage and an equal partnership were considered unconventional, and I heard later that in Hyderabadi circles, my living alone in a barsati away from my parents, determined to live off what I earned, was considered quite weird. A nice young man, coming to check me out as a prospective bride one Sunday morning, was horrified to find me in my dressing gown, without even a maid as chaperone. He had to sit and wait while I ran down to Defence Colony market to buy milk to make him a cup of tea—I didn't have a fridge those days.

Stereotypes change, but a fondness for stereotypes does not. Once it was accepted that I was not standard marriage material, the next assumption (both by those who disapproved and those who envied my lifestyle) was that, as a liberated single girl living alone, I must be wildly promiscuous! In reality, in my 20s and 30s, I lived mostly in my head and in the books I read. Though certainly not frigid, relationships began for me first as an intellectual affinity, then an emotional one, only culminating later into physical bonding. I occasionally admired, but could not emulate, the lighthearted way some of my friends regarded sex. 'Like a fabulous meal—you don't have to fall in love with the cook...' said one. I also had old-fashioned views about messing with other people's marriages, which further curtailed the field!

Family has always been important to me, despite my not opting for marriage. I was fortunate in the security and freedom of a mutually loving, mutually respectful relationship with my parents, who influenced my life and thinking in more ways than I can mention. My cherished mother, the centre of our home, died unexpectedly when I was 30. She was only 58, and my youngest brother 20. I shared our home with my father for the next 17 years, till his death at 87. It was very much the family home; my three brothers, all unmarried at the time, came and went.

Abba remained the most interesting, unexpected, multifaceted, endearing man I knew.

All my life my brothers joked that I was thoroughly spoilt as the only girl among four siblings, a position I greatly enjoyed but hopefully never exploited. With my mother gone, being the only woman in the family took on a different dimension. Totally unlike Amma in temperament, I unconsciously took on some of her roles—hostess, homemaker, letter writer, recipe book, agony aunt, arbiter and adjudicator, an oft-referred to data bank of our extended family relationships and history. I'd always enjoyed cooking and decorating, but (thanks partly to working with craftswomen) I took to embroidery and needlework which I'd previously strongly resisted. I always regret that Amma never saw this, she herself was such a star. I was moved when I found my father, in his late 70s, cataracts in both eyes, sitting on his bed, laboriously but exquisitely darning one of his socks. When I urged him to give it to me to do, he firmly refused, saying he was doing it in Amma's memory; a small acknowledgment of the endless unspoken things she'd done for him over the years.

What happens to other less privileged women without my freedoms? As I work with communities all over India, I meet so many who are trapped in unhappy, often abusive marriages, and others who have sacrificed huge talent and dreams to be at the beck and call of a tyrant mother-in-law,

Over the forty-five years that I have worked in the craft sector, countless young women, whether in Lucknow, Rajasthan, Bengal or Banaskantha, have seen me as a role model for being single. Many have impulsively declared they intend to follow my example. I have needed to gently curb their enthusiasm. The situation for unmarried village women is very different from my own effortless journey. Few can escape from the prejudice and stigma attached to being unmarried, the inevitability of becoming unwanted, unpaid, unvalued domestic labour. Tragically, social freedom for women seems mainly dependent on their ability to be economically independent.

There are some happy exceptions: Archana Kumari who, aged 16, told me one winter night in rural Bihar that she wanted to be just like me. Barely literate at the time, she taught herself English and drawing, joined the National Institute of Fashion Technology, and today runs her own *sujni* embroidery business; single by choice and no longer the talk of her village. Zahida, in Kashmir, took a similar decision. There is Shanta Bai, a young Lambani tribal, who left a loveless, violent marriage and used her extraordinary embroidery skills to carve out a career for herself as a master craftswoman, had an affair and bore a child as a single parent, and has travelled the world exhibiting her art. For most rural women, however, marriage is an inevitable part of life. Like the women of my parents' generation, a kind husband and healthy happy children is their ultimate goal. Most find my singlehood inexplicable and rather sad.

The craftswomen I worked with (though they seldom had a good word to say about husbands), also felt children were a good, indeed necessary, thing. For matter-of-fact practical reasons: 'Who will look after you when you are old…?' Somehow, marrying as an insurance policy against old age was not my idea of career planning. It was never an option. My life was rich and full and certainly not solitary. My mother did tell me that while finding a man who shared my iconoclastic views on marriage might be difficult, I should not miss out on having a baby. According to her, it was the most creative experience one could have.

Despite my mother's encouragement, I was nervous of having a child. I come from a family that would have taken single parenthood in its stride, but I funked it. With husbands you can choose to part company, but with a child who is boring or criminal, you simply have to love and lump it! There is no exit option. What an earth would I do with a child who had no sense of humour?

Fate plays its own tricks, however. I was 51 and long past the thought of either marriage or babies, when a daughter fortuitously came tumbling into my life. We connected quite at random through email (she had a question re Welham, where we'd both studied, though over 25 years apart). This kick-started a voluminous correspondence, after which we eventually met. It seems now as if she has been a part of my life forever. Though Urvashi has her own wonderful mother and family in Madhya Pradesh, she honoured me by declaring me her Amma and coming to live with me. Born a Rajput princess from quite a traditional family, she herself is as unorthodox as this decision. Her father philosophically said it was fated. She came to me, readymade and more or less grown up, so I didn't go through teething and wet nappies.

It's been a fun and (as my mother said) intensely creative time. When Urvashi unexpectedly became part of my life, I absolutely loved it, and took the occasional storm as a challenge. Obviously I had over-thought the burdens of motherhood far too much! Sharing one's life with someone completely different turned out not to be claustrophobic or conflicting, but actually adding an exciting element of surprise and delight.

I have reached that old age now that loving friends feared for me. Life still seems pretty good and not at all lonely. Marriage is not the only form of relationship, and I have had much richness, joy, and companionship over the years, of many kinds, including the surprise package of a entertainingly congenial, incredibly caring daughter (much to the relief of my craftspeople!) As an added bonus, there are dozens of other surrogate children and now grandchildren all over India, who've sat in my lap, imbibing gyan and rejecting it over the years; each teaching me about India's multiple lives and our ever-changing world in their turn.

Meanwhile, as the traditional structure of marriage seems increasingly fragile, fraught, complicated, and often still very unfair, I find it wonderful that concepts of sex, gender, and matrimony are being shaken up well and truly; with both men and women looking at new ways of interacting with each other. New legislation reflects these new mores, just as new combinations of sexes and partnerships are also slowly infiltrating the social status quo, all adding their own spice and variety.

Life is a lengthy business these days, and however one lives it, should be fulfilling and fun, not a cage.

Happily unmarried ever after!

FRENY MANECKSHA

I DO NOT KNOW HOW MANY FISTFULS OF RAW RICE I SUBMISSIVELY swallowed before well-meaning friends and relatives gave up on me. This was rice that would have been carefully picked out by the matriarchs from amid the folds of the bride's sari after the wedding, and distributed to all the young unmarried women. Folklore has it that these grains showered on a bride and groom during the blessing ceremony are auspicious, and will catapult other young Parsi maidens into marriage.

I would hear the priests intoning blessings that had a fair sprinkling of Sanskrit phrases: *laxmi bau* (for wealth) and the inevitable *putra bau* (children, preferably sons), connoting the influence of Indian customs on our ancient Persian rites and signifying the intermingling of cultures. So why, I wondered, did Parsis frown upon those marrying outside the religion? And why did a 'progressive' community cite notions of racial purity and male bloodlines when it came to the institution of marriage? Why were these notions used to justify the strict rules that debar children of Parsi women, who choose to marry outside their faith, from being brought up as Zoroastrians?

I did not have a typical Parsi upbringing because my father was a government officer, posted to corners of India where the

Parsi was a rare species! As a child I was used to people asking
with puzzled expressions, 'Parsi, woh kya?'

But, although fairly liberal, both my parents had let it be
known that it would be preferable to marry within the faith. That
was, in fact, the reason my father actively encouraged me to leave
Delhi, where we were living, and find a job and live on my own in
Bombay. He thought a suitable Parsi boy (*majheno Parsi chhokro*)
would then automatically loom on the horizon. It is to their credit
that although this didn't happen, despite the raw rice I dutifully
chewed, they never put any real pressure on me to 'settle down'
or 'see' boys, although my mother would occasionally sigh and
mumble something about feeling guilty because she had failed
in this huge responsibility!

Truth be told, I had pushed thoughts of marriage into a
dusty and scarcely visited recess of my mind when I stepped
into Bombay as a 22-year-old, and was warmly embraced by its
invigorating ambience of the 1970s. I assumed that, some day, I
would marry so made no conscious choice stay to single—but
marriage plans were always pushed into the future.

My progression into singlehood happened, perhaps, because
I had started enjoying my independence a little too much. Some
relationships had not culminated in marriage. I had consented to
'seeing' a few prospective matches more to assuage my mother's
guilt than from any inclination of mine. I confess I always
returned from the meetings with a sense of quiet relief that it had
not worked out. Maybe it was the wonderful spirit of Bombay
that spurred me into staying single and, despite so many changes,
I can vouch that it is still one of the most woman-friendly cities
in India.

Perhaps it also helped that Parsis have late marriages.
Pressures to get married are far less than in other communities,
and being single is not an anomaly. Today, I am appalled at the

way community attitudes have hardened and calcified, and I am disturbed by some aspects of the Jiyo Parsi campaign. Initiated by the Parzor Foundation and the Bombay Parsee Panchayat, with the backing of the Ministry of Minority Affairs, the scheme began with the laudable aim of tackling the challenge of a declining Parsi population in India. Studies conducted by the Tata Institute of Social Sciences (TISS) and Parzor concluded that this decline was caused by late and 'non-marriages', fertility decline, emigration, by women marrying out of the community, and by separations and divorce.

Some of the initial approaches of the Jiyo Parsi scheme, like offering treatment for infertility and financial help for struggling families to have more than one child, cannot be faulted in any way. But to me, what is disconcerting is the way an outreach programme has been tacked on to address attitudinal change. A publicity campaign with advertisements was conceived to create 'awareness among the younger generation of marriageable age' and to put the onus on young Parsi men, and particularly on women, to marry young and procreate.

Advertisements that are markedly sexist have denounced single Parsi women for being 'choosy' and 'selfish'. Such ads reveal a myopic vision in seeing women solely as baby-making machines. Fortunately the ads have, by and large, been robustly dismissed with hearty laughter or outrightly condemned by many Parsi women. For that matter, an assumption in one advertisement that those who choose to remain single will be lonely and find themselves checking into old-age homes, has been denounced by some men as well!

I also know of Parsi women who have lived in Baghs (colonies where Parsis live that are believed to be the citadels of Parsipannu or Parsihood), who chose nonetheless to assert their individuality when it came to decisions like whether to marry or not. Or whom to marry—whether a Parsi or someone else. They have not let family or society or community influence that crucial decision.

I applaud the courage of Parsi women who have raised the issue of their right to enter temples or questioned the entire theory of bloodline that the Jiyo Parsi scheme endorses, namely that only Parsi men who marry outside the faith can avail of schemes to raise their children as Parsis.

For me the most disquieting note of the Jiyo Parsi campaign is its patriarchal premise regarding the institution of marriage. This has provoked me to ask many questions. Why is marriage considered inevitable for a woman, especially in our cultures? Is our role as women confined to being homemakers and baby-producers? Why are these the only markers of adulthood, with celebrations centred on events like wedding anniversaries, the birth of children and later still, children's weddings? What is this insistence on seeing women as gaining in responsibility and respect only through marriage? Why are women who refuse to conform called old maids, or frustrated spinsters, or people who have not quite made the grade? Is it because Asian societies still tend to be extremely conservative when it comes to sex and relationships?

A few weeks ago, I saw an experimental short film by Rehana Zaman, a Pakistani artist who lives in the UK. Her film, *Tell Me the Story of All These Things* brought together several different narrative threads to examine the social conditioning that affects how we analyse bodies, identities and relationships. One of the threads was a probing interview with Farah, the artist's sister, who spoke of her role as mother/ wife/worker/single woman, and skier.

A revelatory moment is when Farah confesses, with refreshing candour, that for many Asian women, marriage gives them permission to sleep with a man but it doesn't necessarily bring respect. She speaks of her own experience in which her former husband would beat her violently in the day, then expect sex at night.

On my part, I began to experience some of the subtle and insidious attitudes and values regarding my own worth and respect in society as I hit my late 30s and 40s. My sell-by date had passed, even accounting for the late marriages of Parsis. (I use this terminology deliberately to highlight the terrible commodification that is typified in phrases like left 'on the shelf'.)

I recall a pre-nuptial function at which a modern young Parsi woman peremptorily announced that I could not participate in the *mardo saro*, or planting of a mango sapling, a ritual performed to signify fertility, because I was single. I ran off to join the men for a round of drinks and then to eat a hearty lunch! But, yes, it was an ouch moment.

I still encounter attitudes of condescension and pity even though I am now in my 60s. A relative rang to enquire after me in the aftermath of a violent bandh in the state. She added, 'You see, I tell everyone I must think of you because you are all alone!' I had to assure her that I am not really alone, I have good friends who look out for me. Moreover, I think I'm still pretty capable of looking after myself and, as a journalist, have travelled and lived alone in many parts of India.

I get off lightly with just the 'bichaari' tag. It could be worse! It was as a journalist that I learnt of several more abusive epithets—dakini, randi, churail (witch, prostitute)—routinely flung at single women, especially widows, in rural areas.

Perhaps it was my singlehood that resonated and brought forth a huge swell of empathy from the women of the Ekal Nari Sanghatan, an organisation for single women and widows whom

I met in 2006. Initiated by Dr Ginni Srivastava, founder of the NGO, Asthaa in Rajasthan, these women had banded together to fight collectively for their rights.

In conversations with them I understood how, although they hadn't chosen to be single and were married, they were now exercising an active choice in not going down the road of remarriage as a solution to their problems. They derived strength from each other and their collective clout. What was very striking was how they were supplanting families and almost joyfully striking down societal restrictions and taboos, some of them of the kind that I, too, had encountered.

Any woman whose son or daughter was getting married would be draped by her fellow women with the red *chunnari*, and a red tika would be put on her head by her companions in defiance of custom and prejudice.

I also recall the words of one of the women from Udaipur who told me with much assertion of spirit, '*Woh mara, main nahi. Mai adhuri nahin....*' (He died, not me. I am not incomplete ....)

Adhuri nahin. Not incomplete. Over the years this assertion of being complete as a person, of taking pride in one's worth and dignity, and deriving joy from one's own company, has been amplified in my life and in those of my friends. I have reached a stage where I feel blessed and happy with the choices I have made.

There have been many radical changes in the times, too. The recent scrapping of Section 377, the struggle behind that movement and for the rights of transgender persons has highlighted how notions of relationships, what constitutes family, and so on, have undergone many transformations.

Today many young women find it easier to summon up the courage and spirit to choose marriage or not, to live as lesbians if they wish to, or assert their identity as transgenders. I am continually struck by how more women are exercising active choice, how openly they declare their decision to remain single or in other kinds of communities.

Among my own contemporaries, too, life has turned full circle. Divorce, separation, widowhood has brought some of my friends to singlehood again. Others, who had been engrossed with family over the decades, are now suddenly reassessing and reshaping their identities and priorities. In our grey-haired years, we take pride in accomplishments not necessarily linked to the old patriarchal social markers. We celebrate someone's work among underprivileged school children, or the writing of a book, or travelling, or just the pleasure of being in each other's company.

I treasure my morning conversations with S. who has worked for me for more than a decade and been widowed for more than twenty years, as we share a cup of tea or coffee mid-morning. We chat most convivially, with the blessing of time on our hands. One day she told me about her sister called Sakku, who is single and stays all alone in her village in Beed.

'She had a very brief marriage, probably lasted less than a month. She came home and told my parents she was not going back and that was that. She also made it clear that she never wanted to marry again. She has not wavered in all the years.'

How does she manage, I asked, and was told that from a young age, Sakku had worked in the fields, and as an agricultural worker has continued to do so, earning enough for her own upkeep. 'She will manage, she says. We often ask her to come and stay with us but she says she is busy, that she wants to live independently as long as she is capable of doing so,' said S.

After her mother's death, Sakku was forced to leave their home because her brother inherited the house and refused to let her stay on, even though he himself had shifted to another one.

'This was a grave injustice, since out of us eight siblings, Sakku was the one who looked after our mother. Provision should have been made for her to stay on in that house. But our mother never spoke out during her lifetime and Sakku was unceremoniously turfed out by our brother. But the community of villagers came together, and one person who has a small one-room tenement allowed Sakku to stay in it. She lives there alone. She has applied for the scheme in which she is entitled to a house.'

S. recalls that even when Sakku visited her in Thane she was fiercely proud and anxious to pitch in with household expenses. 'Campaigning for general elections was going on in our neighbourhood. Sakku found out that a local party was paying Rs 2,000 to all those who joined up for canvassing. She ingenuously volunteered so that she could avail of the free food, without telling them she was from another village! She roamed around the city with the others in a big tempo, thrilled that not only was she paid for it, but that a day's *kharcha* was taken care of because of the vada paos, tea and biryani that was given to them,' recalls S. with a huge grin.

She adds, 'What is remarkable is that she is always smiling, is generous with whatever little she has and seems genuinely content. She lives with dignity and demonstrates to us and everyone how she has never regretted her choice of living as a single woman.'

I like to think of Sakku and me and many others as those who quietly subverted fairy tales. We did not pine for Prince Charming, wait to kiss a frog, or for a mister to make us complete. Despite all the travails, we live happily unmarried ever after.

I'm not in transit

ASMITA BASU

I MUST CONFESS THAT I WAS FLUMMOXED WHEN ASKED TO write about being single *by choice*. I am not sure, or even aware of, when I made this decision, or if I made it at all. All I know is that I'm all right the way I am. And I'm not in transit.

What writing this piece compels me to do is to think of the moment when I felt all right, but I cannot recall that moment, either. Mine is not a story of resolve and steadfastness!

I was raised in the way everyone is, particularly women— that marriage is inevitable, a must, the only adult state to be in. Growing up, I remember encounters with single people being tinged with a sense of concern, even pity. After all, 'singles' aren't exactly complete.

Looking back I don't blame myself. How else is one to think when every popular story and fairy tale is about finding the ONE. The ONE who will complete your sentences, provide you a secure home, with whom you shall have a family. A family that will look after you when you are old and frail. It all sounded utterly delightful. A knight in shining armour, and later, after my feminist awakening, a gender-sensitive rocket scientist with a brilliant sense of humour.

And I did try, impelled in no small degree, by my grandmother. Having made no progress on the romantic front during my college days, I went through the steps of 'arranged marriages', like my mother and aunts before me. Those were the days before Shaadi.com. So my granny would collect 'bio-data(s)' of eligible boys with missionary zeal. Send them to me. I would then spend many happy hours tearing them apart with my friends and colleagues. She would then read me the riot act and march me off to meet the most suitable boys—usually those referred to by known family or friends.

In my forties, I have only a vague recollection of the ones I met. They were pretty much the usual—some mamma's boys (Bengalis have them in great abundance), some outright misogynists, some liberal misogynists, and some really nice guys. Unfortunately, none whom I wanted to marry.

I have only myself to blame for not finding the ONE. For reasons totally at odds with what my relatives and friends think, of course. For my relatives, it is because I'm too headstrong, 'too independent', incapable of making adjustments. For my friends, it's my uncanny knack for bringing the most desirable of men into the dreaded 'friends-zone'. Perhaps all of this is true.

For myself, to this day, my life's belongings fit into a medium-sized tempo—a *chhoto hathi*, as we fondly say in Bengal. I can pack and leave at any time, and I've never found someone for whom I would give this up.

I must acknowledge that I am extremely lucky to have parents who, while worrying about my lonely, fragile future, have never made any demands that bind me in any way.

Let's, for a moment, turn to this lonely, fragile future that appears to be my lot. Is marriage the only way out of it? At a recent family gathering, while badgering my attractive elder cousin (yes, single people can be attractive), about why she was single, my 85 year-old widowed aunt piped in, 'Why aren't you asking me? Aren't I single? After all those years of marriage. Of course, I'm fine. I do my own thing. I have no complaints. But do I miss someone who understood me? Someone I could share everything with? Independence isn't everything, you know.'

Indeed. I, too, experience my loneliness deeply. I carry it with me. When I'm alone, I resent it for being the high price I've had to pay for my freedom. But I feel it most acutely when I'm with the 'marrieds'. The single state is comparatively constant. Not so the married state.

I have seen first hand how friendships change with relationships. In our 20s or early 30s, when friendships are so easily forged and live-in relationships so new, you are the chief confidante. As the relationship deepens, your friendship also changes. It's not all bad, especially when the children arrive. Limited as my familial roles are, the one I revel in is of being the favourite aunt. And I will do anything to get there. Unencumbered by the responsibility of bringing up a functional adult, I can spoil, adore, bully and incite to my heart's content.

This difference in levels of responsibility is a game changer when it comes to friends with children. There's no competition, really—I've done my time babysitting many much-adored munchkins. Babies are a LOT of work. Toddlers move...a LOT. Then there is school, talents to be honed, illnesses to be comforted. And don't get me started on the teens, they may move less but these dramatis personae can be a handful. While I sorely miss these kids when they leave or grow up, I would probably kill them had I had them with me all the time.

The good thing is that kids bring up their parents well. I have noticed that the well-honed parenting instinct often spills over to single friends. I sometimes find it difficult to distinguish my bestie from my mother! They sound exactly the same when it comes to food, health, home-management, their anxiety about the situation I call my life. The irony is that in my experience, all single people have a nagging/charming (depending on time of day), related or unrelated 'married', who keeps them alive by feeding them and keeping them away from harm.

The world my mother and bestie occupy is different from mine. And while there is empathy and deep fondness, our worlds are alien in key ways. I do not know what it is like to share your space and yourself all the time, and with so many people. I find it a lot less stressful to be by myself. I also wonder at the interplay of conflict and resolution in shared lives and spaces, and the constancy of this interplay. In relationships, conflicts must be resolved since people share the same space. Over time, a pattern in the conflicts and in the way they are resolved comes into being, since there isn't much one can hide in intimate shared spaces. No matter how annoying each other's traits may be, couples gradually condone and accept them. This is very different from the way in which conflicts play out in a single person's life, in which there is always the option to walk away, to leave.

It is in these circumstances that I have found it confusing to be around marrieds complaining about their partners—they all do. When younger, I would jump in and take sides. I am more circumspect now. I have come to recognize this complaining as a coping mechanism, unless it is truly abusive, of course. Tolerance bred over decades is formidably tenacious. A word of caution to young singles—don't ever offer an opinion or take sides when it comes to warring marrieds. It's useless, since your opinion, based as it is on pure theory, is at best utopian, and taking sides always works out badly.

Here, I must pause to explain that my critique isn't limited to the married 'marrieds' but to the whole set who aren't single, but in relationships. The domesticity of the relationships forges similar patterns in sharing responsibilities, inter se, across relationships. While many friends have successfully challenged gendered domestic roles and lived their ideals, I have found them to be the exception. In most relationships gender roles continue, unquestioned. It is to this ordered patriarchy that a single woman, by her very existence, poses a challenge.

This is the basis of stereotypes associated with 'spinsters', the reason why they are seldom heroines in the fairy tales we are brought up on. But my experience of single women has been very different. There is a bond that is easily and almost immediately forged. It is a celebration of life at its most primal and precarious, and in its insistence on giving the lie to uninformed stereotypes. Just as there is bravery and forbearance in weathering the storms in relationships, there is bravery in going it alone.

My point here is not to glorify a single life or denounce all 'marrieds'. Each state has its unique advantages and disadvantages, and one might often wonder, particularly when faced with challenges, whether the grass is truly greener on the other side. My attempt is to draw attention to conversations and attitudes based on assumptions, rather than on an understanding of the uniqueness that makes for the distinction.

The thing is that a single person is not always alone (do not assume that a single state is entirely devoid of romance) and a married is not always accompanied. Aloneness and singleness need not be a matter of choice. Everyone has to face aloneness at some point, even those in relationships. It is just that, compared to the many advantages that 'marrieds' have, single people have more practice with being alone. And just as there is more to marriage than companionship, there is more to singleness than being alone.

Uphill flows the river

BAMA

I AM NOW 60 YEARS OLD. I HAVE LIVED AS A SINGLE WOMAN for most of the second half of my sixty years. This means that not only do I have no husband, children or a family of my own, but that for the last twenty-three years or so, I have been living alone with one grief and pain after another. First, it was the loss of my 28 year-old youngest sister who was killed brutally and buried by her husband, followed by the death, in the following year, of my parents who were shattered by the terrible death of their youngest daughter. As I was trying to come to terms with these losses, my youngest brother, the youngest child of our family, died, or was killed, suddenly, in mysterious circumstances. I haven't recovered from these tragedies, and continue to live alone with these cumulative pains and sorrows. But then, this is the life I have chosen for myself.

I was teaching in high school when my parents started arranging for my marriage. I told them that I was planning to resign my job and join a nunnery. My mother was shocked; she took me aside and asked me why I didn't want to get married. Began to pester me with one question after another, such as: are you afraid of going through the pain of bearing and delivering children? are you afraid that your husband will beat you up? are you in love with someone? Etc. I just kept quiet and refused to say anything. My mother told me then that if I had someone in mind, they would arrange for our marriage. In any case, she told me not to resign my permanent job and make the mistake of becoming a nun. But I was firm in my decision. I entered a Christian religious congregation and lived as a religious sister for seven years. Later, fed up and disillusioned with that life, I left the order and returned home.

Back at home, my parents broached the subject of my marriage again. Once again I had to face the same questions. I had no desire to marry, not because I was scared and frightened of childbirth and child-rearing, or of a wife-beating husband! In fact, in my teens, I had my own sweet fantasies of married life, definite dreams of the kind of man my husband should be, and the kind of loving and intimate relationship we would have with each other. More than this, I imagined how I would give birth to a baby girl like me, and with what delight I would nurse her at my breast, rear and cherish my dear little girl, singing sweet lullabies to her! So I was not scared of marriage in the least. Then, why did I choose to live as a single woman?

I was born the third child in a Dalit Christian household. It was with much struggle and great difficulty that I was able to pursue my studies and become a teacher. My father was in the Indian army, yet even for him it was an uphill task to find financial resources to educate us. You can imagine how difficult it would have been for parents who depended on uncertain daily wages to educate their children. Moreover, neither these parents nor their children had any sense of the importance of education. Their chief concern, understandably, seemed to be how to find the next meal—education did not matter as much to them. I was lucky to have had the advantage of a good education, and I wanted that the new social consciousness and knowledge that my education gave me, benefit my people, too. If I got married, I would be forced to confine myself to the narrow circle of my child, husband and family and be of no use to my people. It was this intense urge and desire for freedom to serve my people that prompted me to give up marriage and opt for a religious life. But I could not continue in that for long with self-respect and dignity, because of the many discriminations that I had to face based on caste, language, complexion (colour), educational qualifications, family wealth and status. So I decided to leave and work for the people without getting married. When my mother and friends suggested that I could serve people equally well as a married woman, it had no appeal for me. The reason was that, by that time, I had realised that the institution and structure of marriage and family as they exist today, are not woman-friendly at all. I knew that in a normal Indian family whose centre is Man—the husband—and his pleasure and well-being, a woman has no freedom and identity of her own. I also knew, equally well, the hardships and difficulties a single woman has to face because she has no male surrogate in the shape of a husband! I liked being myself; I didn't want to lose my self, my being, my freedom and identity, for anyone. With this clarity I decided to live as a single woman.

After three years of training in the nunnery and before we were allowed to take the vows of poverty, chastity, and obedience, we were asked to reflect on why we chose this religious life of renunciation. For this each one of us had to come up with our own list of the pros and cons of married life. I reflected deeply on the positive and negative aspects of both kinds of life. To my surprise, in my list, married life scored better, as it had more positive aspects and fewer negatives than religious life! My Novice Mistress was also equally surprised and asked me why I had then chosen religious life as, rationally speaking, married life had more to offer. I told her that I was renouncing a married life, knowing full well how fulfilling it could be, and opting for a religious life because of a dream in my heart.

I was 28 when I joined the convent. Though I had joined with big dreams, I realised later that a religious life would never give me the opportunities to fulfil those dreams for my people. So, in November, 1991, I left the congregation. Life after that was largely an uphill climb, full of hardship, sorrow, agony, ridicule and humiliation.

Bearing all these (and probably because of these bitter experiences) I wrote my first novel in 1992. This novel, *Karukku*, which introduced me to the literary world as a writer, completely changed the direction of my life. *Karukku* was followed by *Sangati, Vanmam, Manusi* and three collections of short stories. It is this literary life of reading, writing and frequent interaction with university and school students and other activist groups, that gives meaning, energy and joy to my otherwise lonely life. Without these, it would have been nothing but a tale of bitterness, pain, loathing and humiliation. Of course, there were also moments of happiness and delight, which often came as the fruit of my struggles.

After I left the nunnery I struggled hard to find a job, and after I found one there followed a greater and more painful struggle to find suitable accommodation. As I was an unmarried woman and a Dalit, nobody would rent me a house. Finally I managed to get a small room in the house of a Dalit couple who subjected me to indescribable humiliation and restrictions.For those around me in that rural atmosphere, I was an object of unending curiosity as if I were a totally different creature! With great relish, they would dig into the reasons why I wasn't yet married, although I was well into my late 30s, and shared the conclusions of their research with great glee among themselves. Sometimes all this happened in my hearing. Often, when I passed by, I would hear their biting remarks, unsavory comments and veiled jokes about me. If someone in the shape of a man visited me, that would give them a jolly good time to indulge in suspicious banter about me and my morals. Then, suddenly, without giving me any reason or any notice, I was asked to vacate my room immediately. Naturally I refused as I could not make any alternative arrangement. I was subjected to constant harassment by the owners which left a deep and festering wound in my heart. Then and there, I decided to no longer live in a rented place but to have a house of my own.

For me building even a small house as a single woman was a huge challenge. By the time it was built I was completely worn out. As I was building it in the same hostile locality where earlier I had acquired a plot of land, I had to face a barrage of negative comments such as: 'Why a house for her? Has she family or children? After her death to whom is she going to leave this house?' 'She is wasting her money building this house for just a single person. After she builds her house, she should get married; otherwise she will be sitting in her empty house like a lonely owl!' 'In a house shouldn't there be children to run around and play?' Even though I heard these and similar comments, I pretended to be deaf and went about my business with a certain nonchalance. It is true that sometimes these comments angered me, but oftentimes I would just laugh at them. I found it was meaningless to engage in an argument with women who believed that the one and only goal of a person born woman is to get married. So I learnt to carry on with life in silence.

In 2004, I had to undergo a hysterectomy in Chennai. The doctors removed the fibroid together with the uterus. After the surgery I spent a couple of months convalesing with my elder sister in Chennai. When I returned to my house, a few women came to inquire after my health. One of them insisted she should see the exact surgery area and the stitches. I pointed to my lower abdomen where the incision had been made and stitches sewn. She wasn't satisfied. She kept insisting that I remove the covering.

I refused. So she told me that she now believed the talk in the village that was, after all, true—they were saying that I had had an affair with a man which resulted in pregnancy. According to them I had not undergone a hysterectomy, but an abortion! This vile gossip first shattered me and I was on the verge of tears. Then I got furious. I wanted to shout at her and tell her that I didn't have to prove my chastity by showing my stomach to them. I wanted to throw her out of my house. But my feeble physical condition and the pain and mental shock made me helpless. I just kept staring at her for a while and my eyes clouded with tears. But then I controlled myself; I didn't want to cry in front of her. It was all stifled into a sigh within me, wondering why these women couldn't understand the pain and suffering of another woman. The pain of the surgery was less than the pain their disgusting suspicion inflicted on me.

I have found, again and again, that a single woman without much connection to her family is put to the severest test at the time of serious illness. I experienced this when I was reduced to immobility on account of severe chikungunya which lasted for quite some time. Unable to walk, I had to crawl like a baby on all fours. Except for a friend of mine and my younger brother who assisted me for some time, I was left to fend for myself. Though rationally I realised that it was unfair to expect my family, who have their own priorities and preoccupations, to come to my aid at a time of crisis, it could not erase my feeling of utter loneliness and abandonment. When I underwent another surgery for the removal of a large benign tumour, I once again experienced this severe abandoned, orphaned state, as often there was no one to care for me or give me some food. When my parents were alive, I felt differently, felt my mother was always there for me.

My life became a site of continuous struggle and conflict. Gradually, I learned to live with both. A few good-for-nothing fellows approached me in the vain hope that I would succumb to their vile desires because I was living alone. The very sight of these worthless men filled me with a medley of emotions—anger, outrage, fear, revulsion, and helplessness. So I made no effort to make myself physically charming and attractive, and suppressing my gentle character, would go about like a belligerent woman itching for a fight just to scare them off. I often wondered why I had to behave in a manner that was foreign to my nature. But then to protect myself I needed recourse to such pretensions, because during my journeys, especially, I had many, many experiences of sexual harassment.

I know that many women are victims of sexual harassment when they travel. This is a problem faced not only by unmarried single women, but by all women. Once, during a long bus journey at night, a couple was seated by my side. The woman was sleeping soundly in the lap of her husband. I was shocked when I saw this man ogling at me and trying to get my attention! Another time, a man sitting behind a couple tried to caress the lady, and when she shouted, her enraged husband got up and soundly thrashed that fellow. I, too, had many similar experiences. Once I had to slap the driver of the bus who was trying to take liberties with me. Sometimes I would get out of a bus midway. I had to protect myself in such situations, taking into account my state of mind and the circumstances. Whether I was in the house or outside, constant vigilance became my dominant condition as I lived with continuous apprehension regarding my personal safety. The irony of it was that, as I once wrote in a poem, I am a person who wants to live in a house without doors, for whom freedom is my very breath!

As a school teacher, I used to accompany children on our excursions and had to reach the school in the wee hours of the morning. Usually, we returned very late at night and I had to ensure that every child left with his or her parent. I was the last to leave. I dreaded my walk home along a two kilometer lonely road, infested with snakes and haunted by drunkards. It was the same story when the school held a special function that lasted late into the night. I would heave a sigh of relief after I reached home and locked the doors. When a teaching vacancy arose in a village school far away under the same management, our manager wanted to transfer me there, saying that it would be difficult for a married woman teacher to get to school on time. Since I had no family responsibilities I could make it. I resisted firmly, appealed to the higher authorities and had the transfer order cancelled. It was my experience that while others were treated with great consideration, as a single woman I had to fight hard even for my simple rights.

Though I am a devotee of democracy, I dread elections. I go into a state of deep emotional anxiety and tension. Many a time I have had to go on election duty to very remote villages, with no proper roads or even basic facilities. If finding these villages was difficult enough, returning from there after entrusting the ballot machines to the proper authorities, often after 10 p.m., was truly nightmarish. Male officers would go off in their vehicles, while my fellow women colleagues would have either their father, husband, son or brother waiting for them. I would be left alone. On such occasions, for one moment I would almost succumb to the temptation of acknowledging the patriarchal wisdom of Manu who legislated that every woman should be under the tutelage of a man! But the next moment I would shut out such regressive thoughts and summon the courage to find my way home.

On my last election duty I had a very memorable experience. I was sent to a village which had no bus service. Somehow I managed to reach there on time. It was midnight when my election duty gave over and the EVMs were handed over. As usual all my colleagues, both male and female, left, leaving me alone. Seeing my plight, a young man volunteered to reach me to the nearest bus station, which was 30 kilometres away, on his bike. From there I could take the first morning bus to my village. I had no other option since there were no facilities in that village to stay the night. I trusted the humanity of that young man and went with him. It was utter darkness all around as we made our way to the nearest town. He reached me safely to the bus stand. I was so grateful to him that I offered him the honorarium I had received for election duty. He refused, but I forced him to accept. I was at his mercy for almost an hour in total darkness; he didn't harm me, he treated me with respect. I remember him not only for his kindness, but also for showing me another world where men treat women with equity, fairness and respect.

I can never forget my experiences with government officials. An officer would invariably ask me the name of my husband, and when I told him that I had no husband, was living alone by myself, he would raise his head from perusing the file, stare at me, along with his neighbours, as if I was some rare and strange creature! It would sometimes irritate me and at other times exasperate me. I felt like shouting at them, asking them if unmarried women were not human. It was with great hesitation that an officer would put my name down as head of the family on a ration card. It is the same with those who come to collect statistical information. When I tell them that I have no husband or children, they begin to look at me differently. Often, before I can tell them, my neighbours volunteer the information that I have no one, that I live alone. They tell not only these officials, but advertise to all and sundry that I live alone. I am annoyed by this, mainly because such information puts my safety in jeopardy. When I purchase something from a street vendor, some neighbour will say that for a single person like me, a quarter will be sufficient. They decide everything for me because I am single!

I should say that my neighbors were friendly before they got to know me well. On holidays and after I returned from school, I used to sit and chat with them on the street. Sometimes we even played together. They would invite me for family functions and I would willingly participate. As I was financially independent I would help needy people according to my capacity. They, too, willingly came to my help when some need arose for me. When they slowly realised that I didn't abide by their meaningless traditions, didn't follow their beliefs and values, and more importantly, that I am an assertive, self-respecting and proud Dalit, they stopped relating to me. I don't mind that they aren't friendly, what troubles me is their hostility.

However, I know there are a few good hearts who feel for me. It is my deep regret that during the past twenty-five years I have not been able to cultivate a deep and lasting relationship with anyone. Is this the price I pay for living by my convictions and values as a single woman, who detests patriarchy and all kinds of discrimination, and for being a Dalit? Though these regrets and sorrows constantly wear me down, I feel proud of my lonely life, or rather of my life alone. I am satisfied with it and think of it as a life well lived. I hold my head high because there is an undercurrent, a silent river of joy, beneath all the negativities of life, and because I have kept my self-hood and identity. I haven't bargained or compromised with my precious freedom for anything or anybody.

I have a small lovely nest of a home where I can freely sing, dance, laugh or weep. If I wish I can roll on the floor, sleep or take rest. I can cook and eat when I want and whatever I want. I don't need anyone's permission to go anywhere, any time. When I am late returning home, there is no one waiting to find fault with me. I am careful in exercising this limitless freedom with great responsibility, always ensuring my personal safety. For this I have structured a way of life for myself.

My single womanhood has helped me tremendously to be a duty conscious, responsible and devoted teacher. I was never late to school. I took special care to understand the mental and emotional needs of each student, and planned my teaching accordingly. As I was able to create a bond of love between me and my students, teaching was always a two-way process. I have learnt so much from them.

I don't have a child of my own to care for. Maybe that is why I looked upon all my students as my own children and cared for their well-being. It has been my experience that while most married teachers were passionate about the education and future of their own children, they did not show the same care and interest in their students. I dared to speak about it to some of them and the result was that they began look upon me as an enemy. In my leisure hours at home I would think about the children, devising new methods to lighten the class atmosphere, to make learning more enjoyable and easy. I would sometimes make the lessons into songs, composing both the lyrics and the tune, and some lessons into skits. I could do all this because my single life gave me all the time and freedom to do so.

My school was in an area where marginalised people lived. I could help poor children and others who needed some financial assistance freely, as I wished. If I had been a family woman, my thoughts would have been about the welfare of my children and my husband. Moreover, I would have needed his permission to spend my money on others. Now, of course, I have the financial independence to earn money and spend it as I think fit.

More than anything, I have preserved the wholesomeness of my personality without having it smashed to smithereens in a married life, where the ideal is the welfare of the male and the fulfilling of his pleasure and desires. In a society where a woman is considered a doll or a mere commodity who provides sexual pleasure to the man, I live a life that gives me full control over my body, sexuality and feelings. I have happily freed myself from a concept of woman or womanliness that is almost completely conflated and identified with sexuality. Fortunately, my single life enables me to transcend the kind of mechanical life centred around husband and children. It has opened up the possibility of living a free flowing life that is natural and bold, one that preserves one's identity without being artificial or hypocritical. Of course, it has been a very challenging life, full of struggle and conflict, one that has no ready rules nor clear road map to follow, but a life in which one learns painfully by experience. Yet it has been an immensely meaningful and satisfying life.

Instead of restricting myself to the narrow confines of family, caste or religious regulations and ideologies like the average woman, I have been more like poet Bharathiyar's little sparrow which allows nothing to curb its freedom. I have refused to be ruled by the hegemony of these institutions, have aligned myself firmly with forces and movements that struggle for the dawning of social justice and liberation, freedom and human solidarity. My present way of life gives me the freedom and even the luxury of loving and cherishing deeply these values, not compromising with anything that is anti-human.

With Buddha, I believe in the impermanence of all life. My life as a single woman has taught me to love this unstable and fragile life with the freedom of heart, and to live for myself and others. Another blessing this life has given me is the possibility of, and the opportunity to, live in harmony with nature. I wake up to the chirping of sparrows and the soulful song of the cuckoo. I can afford the time to let the rays of the rising sun pour through my window to warm me, and to take the red salute of the setting sun as it makes its descent. The fresh fruits and vegetables from my small garden give me a taste of Mother Earth. In the evening when I walk on my terrace, letting my eyes feast on the green fields below, I am sometimes caressed by a gentle breeze, and sometimes slapped by a howling wind. On a full moon night, I am bathed in her tender light, and on blue moon nights I vanish into oblivion with her.

I inherited all this, I think, from my marginalised people who carry the smell of the earth and speak an earthy language. Probably, this is the precious matrimony that my grandmother and mother bequeathed to me. I must also have received the inspiration and courage to choose to live as a single woman from them. My grandma lost her husband soon after the birth her second child, but that did not prevent her living a cheerful, successful life, boldly facing alone the uncertainties of life, fearing none, extending a helping hand to anyone who needed her assistance. And she was a natural storyteller who could keep her audience spellbound.

Then there was the influence and example of my mother. Soon after their marriage my father left her to join the Indian army. During the thirty years of his military service, he would return only on his annual leave, and lived with us more or less like an esteemed guest. My mother shouldered the responsibility of running the family, giving all of us, their six children, a good education and ensuring that we stood on our own feet. I have seen her and my grandma as individuals who lived independent and lonely lives. Maybe I inherited this trait from them.

All humans have to face loneliness at some time or other. Sometimes it is beautiful and pleasant; at others it can be painful and deadly. Joy and pain are inseparable bedfellows, we cannot avoid them. My mother used to say that if a woman in labour wants a baby, she has to bear the pain! Each one has to find meaning for their own life. The life that I have chosen is certainly full of pain and anguish, but it is a pain that is sweetly life-giving!

Slouching towards singledom

ADITI BISHNOI

I HAVE NEVER BEEN MARRIED. Never quite felt the need to pledge undying love (or semi-servitude, if you're an average Indian woman) in front of a million people, who are only interested in discussing the wedding menu and the bride's weight and fairness quotient threadbare. I've never felt the compelling urge to go in for a secret engagement or even a steady boyfriend (men always, always seem to disappoint after the initial dating rituals)… In short, meet yours truly, a confirmed single girl, who hasn't been able to whip up an appetite for 'grand love' or 'eternal wedded bliss'.

Make no mistake, I wasn't born this way. Like most girls, I've played house (although it was more like camping in the garden and ordering my younger brother do all the 'feminine' chores), I've grown up on healthy doses of romantic fiction and *DDLJ*-esque cinema that promise impossible love set against dreamy backdrops; I've mooned over men; I've been courted… But, in the end, much to my own detriment (as my friends love to point out), I'm too much my own person, unwilling to change or, as I see it, sacrifice myself at the marriage altar. It hasn't been easy being like this, considering that as girls we are constantly being pulled in many different, often conflicting, directions, especially when it comes to matters of the hearth… and heart.

When I first picked up Charlotte Bronte's remarkable book, *Jane Eyre* in Class Eight (the year I came into my own, as a shy but defiant person), I instantly adopted Jane as a role model. Whereas my peers were swooning and waxing eloquent over the intense gothic romance between Jane and Rochester, I spent my teens drawing parallels with Jane's tough journey into womanhood— her determined nature, convinced of her ordinariness, her fierce independence streak—trying to internalise the lessons she taught me about being a working girl (yes, please), of rationally accepting sweeping changes in life (not really), of not allowing a man to have the upper hand or the last word (always!).

A fictional woman became real for me and, to be honest, I've never really got over her influence, even though I've moved on and met many other heroines, both real and otherwise. Every once in a while, when I feel myself being sucked into the overwhelming patriarchal vortex we call society, when I feel I'm chickening out because something is too hard or demands too much from me, when I get apprehensive of the unknown or am wracked with self-doubt, I go back to her because her story provides an independent-minded woman with some timeless lessons. You might wonder why a woman in her 30s would turn to fiction to unravel life, but that's just who I am: an introvert, determined bookworm, convinced that stories do provide real answers to difficult situations and questions. And, obviously, when I got to writing this essay on why I've chosen to remain single, and my take on marriage in twenty-first century India, I couldn't help but recall Bronte's masterpiece on complex love, compromise and marriage.

Of course, Jane found her happy ending—as I see it, she got together with the dashing Mr Rochester on her own terms and at a time of her choosing—and for quite some time I believed (maybe a tiny part of me still does) it would eventually work out in the same way for me. However, my experiences and observations have enabled me to imagine my own life-story with a big dramatic twist—having a happily-ever-after that doesn't include a marriage certificate.

Over time, I have come to realise that I'm surrounded by a myriad forms of love; I have choices; I don't have an obnoxious family that has censured me for my singular efforts at establishing myself as the in-house rebel; I have never been told to be or think in a certain way (the 'acceptable' Brahmin way); I'm not homeless (thank goodness!!!) or penniless (only sometimes!). I already have the freedoms and privileges that my favourite heroine had to struggle for, and so there's no need for me to hyperventilate if I don't ever find my very own Rochester (or Rohan or Rahul). Or maybe I will find different Rochesters at different times of life. And so, marriage is not something I really have to enter to experience romance, companionship, friendship, loyalty... I've arrived at this conclusion on my own, though I'm not sure I'm entirely right, because my theory is untested. One thing I do know for certain: being single is not the catastrophe it is imagined or made out to be, not at all.

Never the ideal marriage material...

I come from a small, closely-knit nuclear family, with a few aunts and uncles, and a handful of first cousins. Fortunately for me, we no longer represent the typical Great Indian Parivaar, with an overbearing patriarch, disapproving matriarch, 'hai-hai' aunties and 'what-are-your-future-plans' uncles; there are no bizarre rules, non-negotiable traditions or any other trappings of parampara. As thoroughly urban Bishnoi Brahmins, my family is neither religious nor overtly traditional. We do try to stay as close to nature as is possible in a metropolis—it's the Bishnois' abiding love for the environment and animals that sets them apart—nurturing a thriving green space in our home, recycling, using renewable energy sources, and so on, but when it comes to following the Hindu tenets we have never been rigid. Life-milestones, especially marriage, are observed relatively simply—none of your long-drawn five-day affairs with tons of rituals and, of course, no hidden dowry agendas. There is, nonetheless, an emphasis on tameez and tehzeeb, which while the older generation was around, was chiefly enforced by the men and upheld and complied with by the women of the family.

When Dadaji-Badi Mummy were around to give their fatwa-like pronouncements and paralyse with their judgmental stares, the home was a silent battleground. They detested loudmouths, believed in brushing almost everything uncomfortable or inconvenient under the carpet, and expected younger women to 'behave' and know their place. Why does she have to be so noisy? Her guffaws can be heard on the road! What will everyone think? Why does she have to run around the house like a freight train? Why does she play on the streets and jump into the nallah when the football falls in? Why is she wearing shorts? Her brother is so quiet and studious, what is WRONG with her!!

Never one to simply bow down to authority, I argued, reasoned, debated, and discussed even the seemingly 'normal' things that were expected of me—and that hasn't changed. Why must the men in the family be served? Why must I always give my brother from my share and not expect him to return the favour? (In all fairness, my brother is a considerate sibling, always willing to share and do things for me.) Why should I not listen to head banging rock or prefer watching MTV to *Mahabharat* on TV! Oh, come on, what's with all the rules! There was—and continues to be—an expected etiquette for girls and women, particularly those from 'good' families, and instinctively I rejected it. But the thing to note here is that while I was argumentative and rebellious at home, outside I was quietly defiant; if I didn't agree with something I didn't voice it, I simply walked away.

From my parents comes my sense of empathy, the attitude to live and let live, never impose, never be imposed upon, think for yourself, learn to connect the dots, look out for one another... in a nutshell, some of what they learnt from their respective parents and a lot more of what they felt they had missed out on. I have also inherited my undying love for books and music from them, and they are my constant companions, my source of joy, my twin lights at the end of the tunnel. As long as I have them, I truly believe I'll be okay. Even if I'm ALONE.

A stroll through the marriage mart

I may not have grown up (or been brought up?) to be ideal marriage material but that's not to say that my parents were free from the pangs and panics of fulfilling their most sacred duty; what, according to the biradari, is the primary purpose of their being around on this planet. *Ek bar ladki 'settle' ho jaye toh chain se mar sakte hain* (once the daughter is 'settled' then parents can die in peace)!

One afternoon, in a bid to establish herself as well-wisher-in-chief, a friendly neighbourhood Punjabi aunty approached my mother: 'I love her as my own, so I'm telling you frankly, please do something about her. You must regulate her food and she desperately needs a rigorous exercise regimen. *Shaadi kaun karega, bhai* if she looks like she will break every piece of furniture she rests her ample behind on, *kitna nuksaan hoga.*' A little (or not so little) secret, I was roughly the size of a young sumo wrestler in those days, and it was the primary occupation of everyone around me to not just fret about my *khata-pita* figure but come up with new, and sometimes downright bizarre, ways of losing weight, with the singular purpose of turning me into a svelte and *susheel kanya*, ready for holy matrimony. From ayurvedic oils, smelly enough to knock out an elephant, to gelatinous Aloe Vera goo, to an RAF exercise manual, to numbers of beefy personal trainers (aah, finally, something worthwhile) and lithe Bharat Thakur power yoga instructors (once, succumbing to pressure, I went for a class where after a round of 100 surya namaskars I bid the world adieu before blacking out, and so that was the end of that), to offers of setting up appointments with naturopaths, nutritionists and wellness therapists (Shikha Sharma, Ishi Khosla, et al), I've sat through hours, weeks, months of well-meant but not well-received counsel, warnings and veiled threats.

Three years of my life spent staunchly resisting these crazy prescriptions and gorging on great food instead (I used to work for a lifestyle magazine and cover restaurant launches and wine tastings as a trainee journalist), and when I turned 28, a malfunctioning gallbladder did what no one had ever imagined: I shed oodles of weight. Whereas I couldn't get over the trauma of a minor surgery, there was a wave of relief and celebration around the block and in the extended family. At last I was presentable enough to hit the marriage mart—and that too at just the right time (*babaji ki meher hai ji*; she's so lucky, na). Things must move fast, advised one, and so my parents asked me, hesitantly, if I thought it was okay for them to go on a groom-hunting spree. They were not particularly thrilled to undertake this search; they'd much rather I found someone on my own, considering my quirky personality, my sarcasm, my obsession with egalitarianism and my deep aversion to sudden change. But as I had not found my person till then (have you met the general crop of men in Delhi, good to go out with but not bring home?), they resigned themselves to giving this uncomfortable drill a go.

Here's how it played out. My parents first dutifully created a profile for me and then went on to shortlist a few of my photographs. My god, what a chore, given the host of instructions and comments—*acche poses honé chaiye, boys ko pata lagna chahiye ki* you are modern but also very traditional, *kuch homely qualities and hobbies bhi list kar dena*, learn to cook at least three Indian dishes(!!)...cringe... Strangely, chemistry and compatibility, which I think should be the cornerstones of a marriage, were not really high on the list. Social status, YES; education, okay; chemistry, what's that; compatibility, forget all this, *sab manage ho jata hai* when you get married!

Together, my parents and I have riffled through letters of interest that arrived by post, scrolled through pages of godforsaken online marriage bureaus (Jeevansaathi, Shaadi, Elite Shadi, Mad About You, etc.), and in one weird phase, even swiped right on Tinder (that was all me). The results of this half-hearted search, and a few 'arranged dates', were hilarious, surprising and even shocking. Man, are men in India set up to think they are god's gift to the human race! Let me present my analysis of a few general specimens I met.

Specimen One: The Mummy Bhakt (my mother comes first, no one can replace her in my life, although the wife must eventually become a mummy clone); Specimen Two: The Trophy-Wife Seeker (the wife must wear branded clothes, be well-groomed at all times, throw great parties and, yes, also have a smart career, preferably in finance, else how will I face the world); Specimen Three: The Pseudo Metrosexual (if ever there is a confused lot, I'm already tearing up with laughter); Specimen Four: Eighteen-and-Immature-Till-I-Die (the less said the better, *arre kitna party aur binge drink karoge*); Specimen Five: NRI Hunting For Desi Bride (maid or life partner, cannot make up his mind); Specimen Six: Because I'm Worth It (take a guess, while I speed dial 100), and so on...

I am not naive. I get that the truth of marriage lies somewhere between my fantasy world—where there's synergy, empathy and sharing, and oodles of romance, obviously—and this cold harsh reality that seems to be the norm. I have several girlfriends who are just 'getting along' in this way, ably investing their time and energies in the home and children because their 'better' halves simply can't be bothered. A dear friend once told me how she thought I was lucky to have the privilege of choice, to have the confidence to be on my own. She said, 'No one lets you in on the redundancy of marriage. For women, there is little to gain and much to lose.' Well, agreed, relationships can't be viewed from the narrow lens of gain and loss but there is some merit in what she believed and lived.

Go, went, gone (case) girl!

Aapki ladki toh haath se nikal gayi (your daughter has gone out of control)! That's the conclusion that most acquaintances drew when it didn't look like I was going to zero in on just any man that came my way. It's really amazing how incomprehensible it is for people to accept anything that is even slightly unconventional. It never occurs to the naysayers that maybe, just maybe, I am a-okay being by myself. That whereas the idea of having a partner (married or not) to share one's life with is wonderful and, in fact, ideal, being with someone merely to satisfy social needs is downright unfair and stifling. It's like subjecting a person to a lifetime of boredom and tedium and there's nothing more tragic than being bored with life.

The thing is, I don't particularly relish change—and marriage brings on the mother of all change. Sure, at the macro level I concede to Heraclitus's change is the only constant, that we are all subjects of change and subject to change. But at the micro level, it's not easy for me to live in flux. I like my life a little bit quiet and a lot balanced (drama is mostly relegated to my imagination), I do not thrive in noise; I have an earmarked space for everything—eating, writing, reading, thinking. I have people with whom I connect with when I want to or when they reach out. I don't like being stalked by humanity 24x7, so none of the frenzied social media posting, tagging, airing of random opinions for me. All things considered, I realised early on that for me to up my everyday and alter life completely, the motivation has to be enticing enough. That hasn't happened. No man has tempted me towards matrimony (even the ones I have had fun being with, briefly dated or felt a little weak in the knees for). So, I have exercised my free will to remain single, in spite of the wide-eyed reactions, the whispers about being a corrupting influence on Gen Next, the fervent appeals to think about the future of the family or condolences at an impending spinsterhood (time *waise bhi nikal hi gaya* now that she's 37).

Alone together, in paradoxical but exciting times

I've noticed that age is a great liberator. As you get along in years, you are not only more comfortable with who you are and what you want from life, but the best part, you don't feel the compelling need to be a people-pleaser. It's a gradual process, one that emboldens and liberates, bit by bit. I've seen my mother, my aunts, and an older cousin sister gradually break free of their shackles and come into their own. It's these strong women in the family who stand by the younger ones, like me and a couple of other sisters who are unmarried, or have clearly stated their intention to skip nuptials altogether. Educated, working, financially secure and loads of fun, that's what our Bishnoi sisterhood is all about—being alone together. In fact, without these critical factors, we know we won't be able to go forward on our own terms. Standing by one another; swapping views on the personal, the political, and the philosophical; and fretting about whether we will indeed be okay—we lean on each other, the married ones and the singletons. Rather lucky, am I not. For, as it turns out, thanks to my family and friends, it's not like I'm really alone.

Despite the support and sisterhood that I enjoy, for me, coming to terms with my choice to give marriage a go-by hasn't been without many conflicting thoughts and emotions. For starters, the irony of not being able to live out my own version of my literature-fuelled fantasy of marital bliss is not lost on me. And then there are several questions, a few worries, and a lot of uncertainty to grapple with on an everyday basis, as I navigate my way around my single status. But I suppose all my concerns are only natural. I often wonder if I'll ever regret being by myself, without someone to grow old with; forever being the third wheel when I go out with friends and their spouses; being the spinster aunt. There is the monumental question of whether or not I'd like to be a single mother; fortunately, there are options available today (biological and adoption) but will I be up for the whole hog, solo? Sometimes, when my 10-year-old nephew looks wistfully at large families, with a battalion of siblings and cousins milling about and asks why he is being denied all this (to guilt me, he wonders aloud on what will happen to him when I'm in heaven; don't I think I should leave someone here for him?) it becomes hard to explain. Given, that for the moment I don't know if I'm cut out for motherhood, or ready to pass on my brand of crazy to a little one.

I also feel terribly uneasy about thinking of a life without my parents. So far, they have been my one constant, my friends, companions and partners in good times and bad. I'm up for the task of being a caregiver when they'll need one, but adjusting to the idea of them gone is unthinkable. Scientists have been able to clone animals, so how about coming up with something that will enable us to hold on to our dear ones forever! Okay, I know being close to Mother Nature and accepting her rules is a Bishnoi thing, but can she please spare the parents! And don't even get me started on my nightmare of hobbling around the house in my geriatric years all by my lonesome self, or perhaps well-ensconced in an old people's home. Again, I'm not sure. What if I run out of money? What about the time I won't be able to read or become hard of hearing? My list of apprehensions is long and loaded but I hope to overcome them in my own time.

If I leave aside my very personal and surmountable concerns about singledom, one thing is very clear: we are living in really exciting times right now, when women are finding their own ways to redefine the age-old idea of womanhood—and, sometimes, they are even successful in roping in men in their endeavours. The 2 Cs of *choice* and *change* that define the way I view and deal with my life-world are also defining our collective today.

When it comes to the question 'to be or not to be… single', there is no one right answer any longer. In fact, if there was ever a time to get married on one's terms, it is now; and if there was ever a time to choose to remain single, it is now. In the weeks preceding this close examination of my single status, it was raining celebrity weddings. Two female superstars (both in their thirties) and a female sports star tied the knot with a partner of their choice, in wedding ceremonies they planned to the last detail, ready to begin a new chapter of their lives, not in their husband's home as convention demands, but in an independently set up 'love nest'.

Their wide smiles and fun, carefree demeanour completely flipped the traditional image of the shy, demure Indian bride, ready to shed copious tears on her *bidai*. I remember a female cousin was strictly instructed not to smile during her wedding rituals lest people think she was happy, and god forbid that a woman should be happy and actually show it!

For many women—mostly well-heeled and financially independent, I concede—marriage, once believed to be the ultimate safety net, is just not that any more. Education, financial security, land and/or property promise much greater comfort and social standing today. While patriarchy has drilled into us the need to seek and depend on 'protection' from fathers, brothers, husbands and sons, we know that's not the case at all. Never was, never will be. (Recall Austen's 19th century wisdom: 'Give a girl an education and introduce her properly into the world, and ten to one but she has the means of settling well, without further expense to anybody.') Choice, another amazing outcome of our slowly changing times, is also a wonderful thing. It has enabled me to look forward to the single life, to not be paralysed with fear at the thought of living without the legal 'buffer' of a male partner.

I think I've yet to live the 'highs and lows' of a single woman's life—my experience till now has been more about gradually making my way towards the singles' road. I'm here now, ready to walk on ahead, but what lies in store for me on this journey is unknown, and, dare I say, exciting. Maybe I'm projecting a bit too much of my rose-tinted naivete, maybe real life will catch up and blurt 'I told you so' in my face—but I'd like to believe that life will find a way to work itself out, whether I'm single or not. And that there is more to me, more to my existence, than being with someone—or not. I refuse to be defined, to conform, to comply… and to change this about me.

A high happiness quotient

VINEETA BAL

A T THIS STAGE, IN MY 60S, IT IS TOO FAR BACK FOR ME TO BE sure of the reasons for a choice that I first made nearly four decades ago. Being single has been the state of my life, happily so, but it is not easy to recapitulate the slow, intermittent and uncertain thought processes that went into arriving at and maintaining that choice. One thing I am certain of is that it was an active choice and preference. I have not looked for anyone to marry and live with ever since I became an adult.

After a certain age, offers of match-making come from family and acquaintances as a matter of course, and my life was not an exception. However, what has stayed in my memory is the first offer. A marriage proposal came my way at the ripe old age of fourteen, at a family wedding. I was told that such-and-such a man, the younger brother of the groom, was attracted to me and would like to marry me! It may or may not have been a serious offer and I certainly did not think seriously about it. Treated it like a joke. But I wonder now whether that eventually helped me stop and think about the institution of marriage and its weirdness. As a growing teenager, I realised that physical appearances, defined as physical 'beauty', are a major determinant of marriage for a woman (apart from the convenient uses of horoscopes!). As a result, I stopped paying any serious attention to either my looks or to my horoscope! Despite there being 'expert' palmists and astrologers in my extended family, their importance for my immediate family was fortunately minimal, as far as I was aware.

When I look back, it seems to me that my family was marginally religious, but not overtly so, while I was growing up. Gods and goddesses had no active role to play in daily matters. Pujas did not happen on a regular basis, though I do remember being scolded and told by a visiting elderly relative to clean all the small idols of gods and goddesses sitting in one corner in the house. I felt very miffed. When we siblings were small children, we were enthusiastic about decorations for the Ganesh puja; the festival was always celebrated, although our enthusiasm rarely lasted for the full ten days. As we grew up and got bored with it, our parents did not insist on it at all. Did this relative open-mindedness contribute to my future choices about marriage? However, it is also true that almost every young and healthy woman in my extended family got married at a socially appropriate age, so conformity was clearly the norm.

Being fond of reading and being a thinking person are not necessarily two sides of the same coin. I certainly was the former, and during my teenage years, grew and acquired some credentials for the latter. Books came as prizes in school, and I remember reading and enjoying them from a very early age. For a long time, I mostly read books in my mother tongue and my school language, Marathi. Thus, Marathi classics, both old and contemporary, more fiction than otherwise, were easily accessible. I realised much later, though, that many of the writers I read in those days were upper-caste men! I also remember reading *Satyakatha*, a Marathi periodical, one of the elite literary magazines published by Mauj publishing house and edited by the legendary Ram Patwardhan.

Many of its authors went on to become established figures in Marathi literature, and it brought many readers like me to an appreciation of the power of modern Marathi writing.

Being able to buy new books was a luxury in those days, so when I found that some new friends and acquaintances had lots of books in their houses, I happily borrowed and read them. Slowly, with my language of education changing from Marathi to English, I began pushing myself to reading English literature. As a result I read children's literature in English in my mid-teens! Curiously, at the same time I was also discovering and reading an eclectic mix of adult writing, both fiction and non-fiction, in English. My reading was shaped by people who would lend me books to read!

By the mid-70s, Gauri Deshpande had become a striking figure in Marathi literature, and her short stories and novels were a major part of my growing up. The women she wrote about were very different compared to those in earlier writing about women, and even by women. Her characters did not necessarily have or lead straightforward linear lives with marriage, children and an uncomplaining acceptance of domestic responsibilities. Influences like this certainly helped me look at married friends and relatives with a more sceptical eye and mind. It struck me, then and now, how many of them continued with their married lives despite being deeply unhappy. In fact, the degree of happiness arising from marriage never seemed particularly high, although of course it varied a great deal!! It was quite evident that the wife was never considered or treated as an equal in most marriages, even relatively 'modern' and 'liberal' ones. Husbands would snap at their wives in public without blinking an eyelid. I have no doubt that such observations were a part of my thinking about my own life and future.

The 1970s, when I was growing up, were also a time of great political and social turmoil in India, with the declaration of the

Emergency, followed by elections that brought about a major change. I was a medical student then, and it was quite apparent to us that many vasectomy camps were being organised in the country. At the technical level, we had learnt and knew that vasectomy can be a very effective and minimally invasive procedure for male sterilisation, much easier to perform than a tubectomy for women. However, after the Emergency was lifted and elections took place, we heard about the gross violations of human rights associated with forced sterilisations in the camp mode, and the morbidity of poor men who underwent the procedure. These concerns were part of my serious consideration of many societal issues that had implications for what I would like to do in future. While these experiences had no direct impact on my choosing to remain single, they clearly affected the choices I made regarding my career and other activities, such as working with women's and science-and-society groups.

Traditional India proudly says that two different families are wedded together via marriage. What this seems to mean in practice is that the families participate actively and deeply in the process, with the unspoken assumption that the bride and groom are not quite capable of thinking independently about their life and future. Unsurprisingly, as a result, child marriage does not seem to be such a great evil; in fact, the involvement of both families is justified, since the bride and groom cannot consent as adults. But while the age at marriage for brides and grooms has been raised, not much else has changed, either forty years ago or even today, in the twenty-first century. I have watched my generation, as also the next generation, getting married in religious ceremonies, although expenses for weddings have steadily gone up. In my youth, weddings in Pune and Mumbai were mostly performed by observing local religious customs, not with the current pan-Indian showcasing of Bollywood-inspired rituals. In my teens and twenties, though I attended such weddings, I became more and more uncomfortable about doing so. I am not sure whether questions regarding my own marriage plans were making me uncomfortable, or whether I was slowly reaching that stage in my thinking when not just the religiosity of wedding rituals, but the idea of marriage itself as a social construct, were beginning to seem like doubtful propositions! In any case, my career provided me with an excellent excuse. I moved out of Pune and Mumbai to London and, eventually, Delhi, leaving all close relatives behind. Naturally, not just the pressure to get married but the pressure to attend weddings, too, practically disappeared.

Looking back, I realise that no direct or indirect serious proposals for marriage came my way after my mid-30s, even from family in Pune and Mumbai. It did give me a sense of freedom, or perhaps relief, for every now and then I had to deal with questions regarding marriage, and try not to upset or seem to insult older relatives. I remember an elderly relative of mine trying hard to find reasons for my being single. I had to provide answers somewhat acceptable to him that would stop the barrage of questions. To avoid further conversation, I settled on saying hypocritical things like, 'I have not come across anybody I find suitable' or 'Not wanting to marry is not a completely foregone conclusion.'

This odd episode of what we might call successful 'self-defence' reminds me of the time I learnt about self-defence as a skill to acquire for living in supposedly dangerous places and situations. A few years ago, a friend and colleague introduced me to Wenlido, a self-defence training method, that actually teaches women how to defend themselves physically, and how to attack an attacker. It taught both physical and mental manoeuvres in countering attacks. By now I have forgotten every manoeuvre I learnt in that workshop, but the self-taught psychological self-defence I often used in response to questions about marriage plans has stayed with me for much longer!

Many women think of being single as an undesirable state. They are afraid of being alone, their families do not want them to live like that. They become the target of ridicule by family and neighbours. Admittedly, the level of social insecurity in staying alone is higher in some cities such as Delhi, but such potential circumstances and situations did not contribute to my decision to remain single.

Staying single is the choice of freedom for me, freedom from many things, both important and trivial at different times. I do not have to deal with a husband who might have treated me as a wife to be ordered about. I do not have to deal with the male ego, at least in my own place and home. I do not need to acquire an additional set of family members as an inevitable consequence. I am not fond of children, and I count the lack of responsibility for children as real freedom. But the basic reality is that this one choice provided me with my own time for myself.

However, I do not think that, as a consequence of making this active choice to stay single and free, I have shirked any responsibilities that I consider properly mine. I have had the space to care for my natal family as best I can. I have had an uninterrupted career, freedom to travel and plan life as I wish, independence in thinking, in making decisions large and small, and executing them.

I have also been able to make active choices about friends. These have not been friends of convenience or circumstance. I have often heard that couples make friends with other couples whose kids go to the same school, or have children the same age as their own, and so on. These sound to me like friendships of convenience. I did not need these; instead I actually found people who find each other mutually interesting and worthwhile. It is no surprise that these like-minded friends of mine are, more often than not, single! A circle of friends for whom I care and who care for me, can be considered a 'family', though the word carries too many restrictive social connotations for me to be comfortable using it. As age advances and debilities increase, I might feel the need for help and support; but is that not what friends are for? Besides, it is also a common experience in many families that sons and daughters who were supposed to be the support system in old age are miles away, quite often outside the country, and sadly, of no real help.

I was lucky that the frequency of questions about marriage from my extended family reduced as I moved out of the familiar surroundings of birth, education and family, but other experiences which single women face do not disappear. It seems no culture is immune to the consequences of being single. A recent article in the *New York Times* by Glynnis MacNicol titled 'I'm in My 40s, Child-Free and Happy. Why Won't Anyone Believe Me?' reminds us that men are after all men, with all the privileges of patriarchy. I wonder what the status and experiences of single women are in the few scattered matriarchal and/or matrilineal cultural pockets around the world.

Despite my formal training as a physician, I have worked as a research biologist all my working life. During medical college itself, I noticed that there were very few single women among the teachers in my college, as well as among practitioners of medicine. I realise that I am not even sure if the proportion of single women in such professional careers is larger or smaller than in the community in general, so many of my comments henceforth will perforce be about all women, rather than only those who are 'single by choice'.

Regardless of whether they are married or single, women trained as physicians who make careers in medicine, still tend to prefer certain specialisations. For example, finding women in many surgical disciplines is uncommon, although gynaecology-obstetrics is an obvious exception, as is ophthalmology, and as a related discipline, anaesthesiology. Even within the medical college teaching faculty, pre-and para-clinical departments saw, and still see, higher proportions of women teachers than in most clinical departments. Patriarchy, including but not limited to marriage and subsequent 'adjustments' in life, likely contributes to such choices, then and now. In my student days, the number of women students taking admission to government medical colleges (it was mostly government medical colleges in the 1970s; medical education and running hospitals was not such a booming business then) was relatively high, certainly 40-odd per cent, unlike engineering where it would be closer to four per cent. Again, those were the days before 'information technology' became a buzzword and women could become IT engineers more easily than civil or mechanical engineers. However, then and now, all these professionally trained women faced, and continue to face, the pressure of impending marriage, which actively or passively influences their choices of not just careers, but all aspects of life.

After starting work in New Delhi in 1990 as a faculty member and an independent research investigator, it struck me afresh how few women there were around me as faculty members. The numbers I knew in the life sciences, though small, were apparently still much better than in other natural science disciplines, especially physics and mathematics. I used to hear stories about how there were no toilets for women in the whole building in some very well-known Indian research institutes. I was in a better place, I suppose, perhaps because it was newly established.

Two other related things were new for me. First, campus housing, which had its advantages and disadvantages. I did not have to face the challenge that some of my friends did of finding a decent place to live in. I did not have to use public transport in Delhi on a daily basis. On the other hand, it was easy for everybody working with me to notice and comment on my visitors—men or women, young or old, relatives or friends—and this felt distinctly different where a single woman was concerned.

Second, I began experiencing the patriarchal attitudes of men in authority directly, without the buffering or filtering provided, sometimes unwittingly, by a research supervisor or advisor. Again, I am sure that this is a common experience for all women in an academic career, whether married or not. My feminist perspectives and my connection with the Indian women's movement, both of which predated my academic career, helped me deal with the patriarchy at work. Despite some early instances of what felt like gender-based discrimination, and an occasional situation that felt, more clearly, like sexual harassment (predating the Visakha judgment which provided a vocabulary for it) I managed to work in relative peace. However, I think I did acquire a reputation as someone who would speak up on women's issues, especially on discrimination. These comments did not necessarily go down well in male majority committees and other such gatherings. I don't know how often this reputation of mine was the reason to subtly drop my name from various committees. One never knows, but in any case I have no regrets.

After settling down in my formal job as a faculty member, I looked for a women's activist group where I could work as a volunteer. I found one, and before long became an integral part of it. This association helped me in many different ways. In addition to clarifying and strengthening my feminist perspectives, it gave me a clearer awareness of gender inequality in professional fields.

As a biologist and experimentalist, it seemed natural to me to look for data about gender inequality in my field. There was hardly any evidence available from Indian academia, though there was some from developed countries. One thing led to another, and I got involved as a foot soldier in some efforts directed towards a better understanding of the status and gender-specific problems of women scientists in India, and in developing recommendations to help improve matters.

As is seen in many other professions, women lag behind in their academic careers when compared to men. Most women themselves take it as their fate, or as a part of their lives, a compromise they need to make for the good of the family, and so on. This secondary status is so deep-rooted that even when women scientists in India came together to form the Indian Women Scientists' Association (IWSA) in 1973—predating the establishment of women's studies as a discipline in India— the issue of the prevailing unequal status of women scientists never really found a strong voice in it. While their mandate is 'Understanding the problems of women in sciences and to be a representative body of women in S&T', the reality seems to be that the founders came together with the main idea of fulfilling their social responsibility to take science to the masses. That is certainly a worthy cause. But it is striking that women scientists do not, and did not, think as intensely about contesting the inferior status of women in the workplace, in the family, and in society. I wonder if gender compromises go so deep for married women, even more than for those single by choice, that they do not really see the consequences of patriarchy on women's lives. Without a clear-eyed vision of gender politics, it is impossible to think seriously about any change.

However, it is also true that when prodded, women scientists do notice and begin to speak about the discriminations they face.

As a member of the task force for Women in Science set up by the Government of India in 2005, I had the opportunity to meet many women scientists in different parts of the country. When the mandate of the task force was explained and discussions initiated, many women talked about the gender-related difficulties they faced while working as scientists. Of course, one meeting or interaction does not go anywhere in terms of making an impact or bringing about change. However, it was very apparent that they were noticing problems, but not voicing them. Most of the women scientists we met were married and they had to either stay put in a place not of their choosing because of the husband's job, or had had to move from place to place for the same reason, resulting in frequent career breaks. It was so rare to find a never-married woman scientist in these gatherings that I began to wonder—are never-married single women scientists so few?

A survey conducted by the National Institute of Advanced Studies (NIAS), Bangalore, in association with the Indian Academy of Sciences (IASc), tells an interesting story in this context. Along with other colleagues, I was part of the group that conceptualised this survey; its results were published in 2010 as 'Trained Scientific Woman Power: How Much are We Losing and Why?' As far as I know, this is the only survey which has interviewed and collated data on women scientists in India, both those who have continued in their profession, and those who have have left it. The survey also includes men.

Data indicated that 13 per cent of women trained as scientists had never been married. In contrast, only two per cent of men interviewed were single. Among women currently pursuing research, the proportion of the unmarried was marginally higher at fourteen per cent. While the sample size was small, the evidence does indicate that more women than men scientists are single. The 2011 Census documents the frequency of men of all ages who claimed to be single (never married or widowed, divorced, separated) at nearly 55 per cent. The number for women was somewhat lower, at 51 per cent, but the difference in frequencies between the two is not stark.

While these data cannot be extrapolated easily to the age-group of working men and women, the question is: is there an advantage to being single as a practising scientist? Conversations with women scientists, both in task force interactions and during this survey, repeatedly indicated that women do feel that looking after children and the elderly in the family and shouldering household responsibilities, ties them down and creates hurdles in pursuing their profession efficiently, and to their own satisfaction.

In this context, I must confess that I think my own decision to remain single by choice contributed a great deal to the happy pursuit of my career. Being single has been a very happy state in my life.

A fine balance

RHEA SARAN

LET ME START BY SAYING I'M NOT OPPOSED TO MARRIAGE.
Quite the opposite. I've always viewed marriage as a sacred
thing. Odd, you might think, considering my own parents got
divorced when I was three years old. But, if anything, that only
made it all the more sacrosanct in my head. I remember thinking
as a teen, that when I married it would need to be for keeps.

Obviously there are no guarantees. A fact amplified by
the unions around me where I've seen fissures, resulting not
necessarily in divorce, but in varying degrees of unhappiness or
apathy. Just because you want a happy marriage doesn't mean
that's what you're going to get, or at least not all the time. No one
can predict how time and circumstances may change two people.
There are, of course, happy marriages in my circle, too—my
absurd optimism about the institution would be harder to keep
up if they didn't exist.

My firm belief in the relevance of marriage might come across
as old-fashioned. After all, women today don't *need* marriage in
the same way our predecessors did. (Let's quickly acknowledge
that this is only true for women of privilege, of which I am
one.) Thanks to socio-economic and political advancements,
for the most part, women have choices and rights. Women can
work. Women can choose not to have children. Women can

be economically independent. Women can remain single. So far, I appear to have made most of my choices as those prone to stereotype would think the daughter of a respected feminist would: I work, I'm economically independent, and I haven't (yet) married.

But this has nothing to do with making a statement. It just so happens that work—and a life that's taken me from Bangalore to Hong Kong to New York to Mumbai to Dubai—has been in sharper focus thus far. And during this time, I simply (and it really is quite simple) haven't met the person who would be a good life partner for me (and vice versa).

Yet none of that diminishes the fact that I still believe in the fairy tale. Or at least a fairy tale tweaked for the twenty-first century: Girl meets Boy. They fall in love and get married... because they share great conversation, trust and companionship, similar life values, a satisfying sex life, respect for each other's work and independence, a mutual desire to procreate, and families that aren't too crazy. And when, after a year from the birth of their first child, Girl decides she wants to go back to work (because, let's face it, she's something of a powerhouse). Boy is supportive, because her strength and drive are part of why he fell in love with her in the first place. And they live happily ever after.

Therein lies the snag. In the tweaking of this tale. I am not 'single by choice' because I don't want marriage—I have always been more than open to it—but I do believe that in order for it to remain relevant and attractive, especially to women, we need to update the relationship balance inherent to a marriage.

Despite societal advancement, marriage has, for the most part, remained deeply patriarchal in many countries. Socio-religious rituals continue to enforce this. A woman is walked down the church aisle by a man and then 'given away' to another man. Which is not unlike the Hindu ritual of kanya daan, and the traditional idea that once a woman is married she belongs solely to her husband's family (men don't have to forsake their birth families when they marry). In some cultures, a woman even changes her first name after marriage—which has always amazed me, because surely your name is a key part of your identity in the world. For a writer like me, my name means everything.

The marriage ceremony is only the start. Men, too, are pigeon-holed by societal expectations in a patriarchal society. A recent article I read talked about why South Korean men are staying unmarried—there, apparently, a man feels he cannot take a wife if he can't afford to buy a house, and given the state of the world economy... enough said. That line of thinking, where the financial burden is placed squarely on a man's shoulders by society, is common in plenty of other cultures, including South Asia. And it is deeply ingrained. I have yet to meet a desi man who'll comfortably let a woman pay when they're out together, even for something small, even occasionally. Don't get me wrong, I enjoy, and am appreciative of, being treated, yet it's also nice to periodically have the opportunity to return the favour. I once bought lunch for a man I'd dined out with on a weekly basis for years, and he was so uncomfortable that he brought up 'the incident' several times. Needless to say, it never happened again.

And let's not get started on familial expectations of a woman after marriage, from home-making to (often solo) child-rearing to general service to the in-laws, in a way that men aren't expected to reciprocate with her family. All of which is designed to cut down the kind of time and opportunity she would have to work or pursue any other ambitions, goals or dreams of her own.

At this point, I'd like to make it clear that I do plenty of home-making entirely willingly as an independent woman—I love to cook, for a start, and there's something very satisfying about finishing a load of laundry—and I very much want to rear children. If that means I will one day have to put my career on pause, I would do so in a heartbeat. You wouldn't need to ask me twice. But it would be a choice I make, not an expectation foisted on me.

As a woman in the twenty-first century, my definition of a successful romantic relationship, and thus of marriage, is about partnership, in the truest sense of the word, and about both partners having choices. It's about a fluid sort of equality that swings one way or the other at different points of time, and in different situations and aspects of life. It's about there being a balance. Yet, in my experience, the closer I, as a woman, get to this levelling of playing fields, the less comfortable many men I encounter seem to be with the scenario.

Why is that? What is it about self-confidence and success in a woman that is so daunting? Why is parity in a relationship so scary? Is it because while we've focused as a society on the upliftment of women over the decades, we've forgotten to bring men along for the ride? That innately patriarchal societies see any strengthening of a woman's position as a weakening of their own? That, as we empower women, we've neglected to change the original narrative, confusing men who were brought up to believe one thing about their place in the social order, but are facing a different reality.

I'm not a sociologist. All I know is that the fairy tale often falls off a cliff way before the ring ceremony. You see, Boy does fall for Girl in part because of her drive and personality and ambition… but then he has enough of that. Every word Girl doesn't hang on to, every new feather in her cap, every business trip she goes on, every independent thought or action, every time she chooses to do something for herself for a change, it all adds up to the inevitable conclusion that she simply wouldn't make a Good Wife. He fails to recognise that in a world that's evolved, wanting and *choosing* to be with him when she doesn't really *need* to, is actually a far stronger ego-stroke for him.

And, frankly, Girl finds Boy's lack of confidence and caveman-era instincts unattractive. Surely only animals in the wild still need to enforce that alpha dominance. (And even there, the lion is a handsome, no-good layabout while the lioness is the breadwinner. Still, he sticks around, you don't hear him asking her to sit back and watch him hunt.)

There is a mistaken belief that a woman who is feminist, and is ambitious and successful and believes in equality of the sexes, cannot also possess the more 'womanly' traits. If she's a 'career woman', she's unlikely, so they seem to think, to spend any time in the kitchen. Or be a good mother. Or be adjustable and available and kind. Clearly they didn't grow up in my home. My mother by all definitions is a feminist, yet my stepfather has never cooked a meal for himself. She loves the kitchen, it's the biggest room in their new house. And a good mother? Available, adjustable and kind? She gave up an editorship to work flexibly in order to be home for me as I was growing up. (And yet she still has an active career now, in her mid-60s.)

Perhaps the only way to update the definition of marriage for this century is to update the definition of what it means to be a woman, to be womanly, a career woman, a feminist, a wife, in the male lexicon. It's currently past its sell-by date for the world we live in. When society recognises that being ambitious and being a good mother aren't mutually exclusive; that loving your professional life and wanting a personal one doesn't have to be an either-or; that reaching for the stars doesn't mean you can't be down to earth (and that this is true for both men and women) only then are we close to looking at the genders as equal.

This is important, because as long as men aren't socialised to accept women as their equals in life, it's increasingly difficult to see how current and future generations of women are going to agree to enter into the marital contract as it stands now. Women are (slowly) being made true partners in businesses the world over. Why wouldn't they want that at home?

I'm an optimist. I firmly believe that there are men out there who have recognised the sea change and are riding that wave alongside women, with confidence and respect. I hold out hope that one of them will ride my way soon.

Single—and free

SHERNA GANDHY

MAYBE, ONE DAY, A BOOK LIKE THIS WILL NOT BE NECESSARY. It will not be necessary to explain this extraordinary phenomenon of being 'single by choice' or at least 'happily single', because it will have become common, maybe even the norm. Who knows? Apart from this not being too good for the human race's chances of survival, such a radical shift is still light years away and, as of now, the status quo of marriage, husband and children is still considered a woman's most correct and necessary manner of existence, though it is under challenge.

Very few women actually decide, right from the time they are of marriageable age, that they will not get married. Most of us think it will happen, so powerful are the messages we internalise from everything around us. If it doesn't, it is for a variety of reasons, all personal to the individual, yet with some common threads.

As the feminist Gloria Steinem believed at one time in her life, I, too, thought that marriage was inevitable, but felt I would be quite clever if I managed to avoid it. Looking back, I realise this was probably an unusual way of thinking as a young adult, when the pressure is on to get married and settle down. At least that's how it was in the 1970s when my peers were getting hitched by the age of 23; by 26-28, the age at which urban women today think seriously about marriage, one was considered to be well over the hill.

The fact that many women today are marrying when they are much older, is already a sign of change. Completing their education, which goes well beyond the twelfth standard or even a BA/BSc, is quite common, and that leads to a job which delays marriage till one's late 20s, at least.

To understand 'singleness' in India one has to look at the social, economic and political dynamics at play in a particular region or community. One of the most compelling reasons for women to marry in our society, whatever the region or community, is undoubtedly family pressure. Parents are desperate to get their daughters 'well settled', an euphemism for getting her off their hands, and it may be difficult for many girls to withstand that pressure, even if they want to.

The dynamics in my family and community made it easier for me to stay single. Except for the odd niggling relative, my family put no pressure on me to marry. In my Parsi community it was not uncommon for women to remain single—my grandfather's two cousins were 'spinsters' and no less respected for that.

Certainly, for a very small community, it was necessary to grow the numbers so an unmarried woman should have been regarded as something of an outcaste. In the distant past this may have been so. But from at least the third decade of the twentieth century, Parsi women were being educated in increasingly large numbers (we are a primarily urban community, concentrated heavily in Mumbai), and by the 1950s and 60s were holding down jobs, which may have made marriage less inevitable. I also think that our parents are quite supportive and allow unmarried daughters to live in the parental home quite comfortably. This is not the case with women in many other communities who are made to feel unwelcome in their natal homes if they remain unmarried after a certain age.

So, in a way, for me to remain single was really very easy. My parents encouraged me to study, and I was 25 when I finally quit accumulating degrees and started working. Marriages are not 'arranged' in my family, at least there were none in my generation, and not even for older cousins who all found their own partners. Arranged marriages were the norm among Parsis at one time, and there are still 'gatherings' of marriageable young girls and boys today, arranged by some community organisation or other. But 'love marriages' were never taboo; there was disapproval only if one of the couple was not of the same social or financial standing. Since there are no caste or regional differences among Parsis, that aspect does not enter the equation.

However, until quite recently, marrying out of the community was the big no-no, particularly if it was the girl who was marrying out. It was a matter of shame to do so, and those who did were barred from entering temples, sometimes disinherited by their families, and their children not be considered Parsis. The last still applies, mainly to women, on the erroneous and paternalistic assumption that children of Parsi fathers married to non-Parsis are more likely to imbibe Parsi ways and culture.

For a tiny and very distinctly different community which does not allow conversion, it was essential that its numbers not decrease; marrying out of the community would not serve that purpose. That the law should change in keeping with the times is something that a deeply conservative section of the community, and much of the clergy, will not accept even today, though the number of Parsis now marrying out of the community is huge.

There is a hard-core section within the community that still shuns marriage to a non-Parsi, but most young Parsis today don't think of this as a barrier. Living, as many of us do, in cosmopolitan, mixed neighbourhoods in cities like Mumbai or abroad, community pressure is minimal and, anyway, the Parsi clergy does not have the kind of heavy-handed authority that clergies of some other religions do. Most do's and don'ts are not prescribed in any religious text, they are just a matter of practice. The discrimination against women in the matter of interfaith marriages has been challenged in court by a woman, born Parsi, who married a non-Parsi, and demanded that she be allowed to be present during her parents' funeral rites.

Women going out to work was the norm for my generation. Many of my relatives were quite helpful in finding me jobs rather than devoting their energies to hunting for a suitable marriage partner!

I managed to pay my own way on a very modest salary, although living in the parental home I had no worries about money for rent and food. Cities are expensive places to live in and financial considerations do push women into marriage, even today. To be free of that removes another support from the institution of marriage. As paid employment becomes the norm for urban and semi-urban women once they complete their education, it is easier to withstand the pressure to conform and marry, if you have no real desire to do so.

Though mine was not a conscious decision to not marry, this was the late 1970s and feminism was very much in the air. I was very conscious of the inequalities that marriage definitely confers on women, and resented it. I had no great desire to have my own home, but I would certainly have had children had I married. Again, that was not some great urge that had to be fulfilled, but children outside marriage would have been a little too much even for my liberal family to accept, and I myself did not have the guts to take on such a responsibility on my own. For me, in my circumstances, it was easy to remain single.

But what about romance or falling in love, a very compelling reason to marry? Nothing to be done about that, of course. If it happens, it happens, but it didn't happen seriously with me. Not that I didn't have romantic imaginings. A large number of women are, or at least were in my time, perusers of romantic serials and such like. In my teenage years I devoured the romances I read in back issues of an English women's magazine, *Women's Weekly*, that my aunt who lived in England, sent us periodically. These were not exactly Mills & Boon, but close enough. Women had careers and minds of their own in some of these stories, but ultimately succumbed to the taciturn charm of the hero. Jane Austen's more pedestrian heroes also played no small part in my imaginings, and Charlotte Brontë's Rochester and Jane Eyre were objects of youthful admiration—though I drew the line at something called The Sheikh, much beloved of my grandmother's generation, about a beautiful, headstrong English aristocrat who was kidnapped by a dashing Arab sheikh who lived in the desert, fell in love with him, and was suitably 'tamed'. Peter O'Toole as T. E. Lawrence in *Lawrence of Arabia* was drool-worthy, but one did not seriously expect Hollywood heroes to be incarnated in Bombay boys.

Being a voracious reader, what I read undoubtedly influenced me. Maybe it was the impossibility of finding a flesh and blood hero who measured up to the fictitious ones that saved me!

Since I never met anyone I really wanted to marry, devoid of the pressure to do so, and in a job I liked that entailed long working hours, I did not feel at odds with my situation. As time went on, although many of the girls and women I had known in school and college did get married, a fair number didn't, so, again, my single status wasn't so remarkable.

Television, films, and advertising give one the impression that everyone is hell bent on getting married, but the findings of a survey of unmarried American women in the 35–45 age group published in *Psychology Today*, who were asked to prioritise what they most wanted in life, shows this isn't the case. Top of the list was a home of their own (44 per cent), second was advancement in their jobs (34 per cent), and third was financial stability. Marriage was a distant fourth. The outcome may be much the same for educated urban Indian women if they lived in a slightly more liberal environment where, for instance, they would find it easy to rent an apartment instead of being subjected to suspicious glances from watchmen, neighbours, and even the managing committees of housing societies. The director of the film, *Bachelor Girls* recounted her own experience of being made to feel so uncomfortable that she finally left the apartment she had rented. An unmarried girl living on her own, even in a cosmopolitan city like Mumbai, could be seen by the censorious as being 'fast', even though she has to fight off male predators at work and on the streets. Of course, in more conservative societies, the outcome would be very different, though we are beginning to hear of girls in rural India preferring further education to early marriage, and even refusing to get married at an early age.

A satisfying job is very important. I wandered into journalism by chance, but found it suited me very well. My first job was with the women's magazine, *Eve's Weekly*, which was undergoing quite a change from being a traditional women's magazine to talking about women's issues such as rape, dowry, domestic violence, the portrayal of women in the media, and so on. This was the early 1980s and it was an interesting time to be in journalism, with new publications starting up, meeting people with like-minded ideas, and attending feminist meetings. The work environment was particularly attractive—we were all women on the editorial team and got on well together, and are friends even today. No one worked overtime, Saturdays were off (rare for any publication) and three months maternity leave was given long before it became mandatory. Other jobs I moved on to were more demanding, entailing long working hours, as is common in the profession. Most of the staff at *The Illustrated Weekly of India*, my next job, were unmarried, or married but with no children, and thus able to cope with a 14- or 15-hour work day.

Many women cope admirably with a job and the demands of home and family, but it calls for the kind of multi-tasking I am not good at. Giving up my job for marriage was not an option for me, though it is a choice many women have to make. Some take to working from home, others go freelance so that they can choose their assignments.

A satisfying job may well stand in for marriage, but the converse may be true, too—not having a job or profession one likes could make marriage an attractive proposition. I was lucky that I liked my work, and concentrated all my energies on it.

Of course, there is a tendency among people to believe that if you are single, you must be terribly unhappy (some may even wonder if there is something 'wrong' with you). Being in a relationship can be lovely, no doubt, but there's enough evidence that marriage is not all it's cracked up to be, that, often, it is a compromise, and the one doing the compromising is the wife. As a single woman you are free of this constraint, can do what you like, stay up till four in the morning, eat what you like, meet whom you like, socialise and travel. Don't like going to a restaurant or movie alone—go with a friend or friends, many of whom are also single or divorced, and happy to form a 'girl gang'.

If all this sounds selfish, perhaps it is. I see it as the upside of being single. And it's not *really* selfish. Women are often the caregivers or support for their elderly parents, and if you are single you usually assume that responsibility more readily than a married daughter or son who has her/his own family responsibilities. Ah, but what about when you grow old and need the support of spouse and children? In India, children are still supposed to look after their elderly parents, particularly financially, in the absence of any social security. I admit that someone to take care of you when you are old and ailing is an attractive proposition, but kids now are more likely to have settled abroad, paying no more than bi-annual visits home. Old age communities are springing up now for just this purpose and, in time, will be comfortable places for the elderly.

I really believe that if the social pressure to marry—amounting to harassment in some families—is left out of the equation; if women have financial independence and are confident that they can manage their lives on their own, marriage will not be inevitable for them. They will have a choice, something that women are all too often denied, in everything.

Life around a hearth, away from home

AHELI MOITRA

GRATED MANGO HOT-AND-SWEET CHUTNEY, AMLA-MUSTARD pickle, *aloo porotha, roti, palak paneer, motorshuti'r kochuri, aloo'r dom, chiwda, chakli, bhakadwadi*, dry fruit, chocolate. I was returning to Nagaland after spending Christmas and the beginning of 2019 with my parents in Vashi, Navi Mumbai. My mother carefully planned, cooked and fed me what she could in the time I was at home—an annual visit—and what she could pack for me to take back to where I lived and worked, on the eastern periphery of the Indian subcontinent.

Mother was prepared. She had already fed me *chingri maach er shorshe-malai* curry, *kosha maangsho, patla maach (ilish, rui, catla, pabda) er jhol, kolai er daal, shukto, aam daal, posto bhaja, aloo posto, shahi paneer, keema, gur er shondesh, rosho puli* and some more, in less than a week. For the rest, she had food boxes, scotch tape, ziploc bags and newspaper. For almost fifteen years, she had managed to feed, care for and sate the Bangali food cravings of her two daughters, constantly on the move. Father had, likewise, adapted. Like temple trips, my sister and I were required to visit our banks, discuss fresh investments, sign requisite documents, get medical check-ups, and shop. One day would be set aside for meeting Father's colleagues at his office in the daytime; the same evening slated to honour Mother's group of friends at the park where she walked, air-gymmed and communed every evening. This is where the silent agreement between my parents and I got prickly. Everyone would assume I was the married daughter settled in New York; in other words, the older successful one who would naturally be followed by the younger one, by example.

In our case, my sister, Masoom, younger by four years, is a community urban planner, consultant faculty at the Parsons School of Design, activist and artist in New York City, married to Umesh, a software engineer, sarod maestro and painter, among other things. I am a journalist in Nagaland for a local newspaper, *The Morung Express*. My parents' colleagues and friends are aware of the details but somehow confuse the order of life, also due to the uncanny similarity of mannerisms between Masoom and me. At the office and in the park, people stand up to greet me, smiling broadly, hands stretched out to shake, to hear about all they had already heard about New York City and the encumbrances of married life. What they hear is, 'Oh, I'm the older one. Journalist. Nagaland?' Eyebrows furrow, hands withdraw. 'Journalist in Nagaland?' Heads tilt. People sit back in their armchairs and park benches. 'Oh, so you are the younger one?' some assume, hoping the job is a hobby. Others, every year, ask, 'Are there terrorists there? What do they eat? What do you eat? When will you come back? When will you get married?'

I am 34, and after years of household turmoil, have stumbled upon a smooth relationship with my parents, after December 2016, when my sister married and, inadvertently, took pressure off the manhunt my parents had launched on my behalf. Ever since I turned 25, our relatives and peers hoarded the burden of five-more-years-of-marriageable-age-left on me; by the time I turned 27, my parents began to panic, engineered profiles on Shaadi.com, Bengalimatrimony.com, even became Facebook friends with prospective grooms, who eventually moved on and married other people. Parents looked at their wedding pictures and lamented. Relatives offered their astrological expertise to see what the stars had 'in store' for me, the ominous signs that were responsible for my continued singlehood. One forecast predicted lifelong stomach issues, another declared I would become famous in 2014, marry 'lately' and become a 'womaniser'. I still struggle with stomach issues, 2014 came and went like the other adventurous years, and I befriended more single women over the years (I wouldn't call that womanising!). The astrologers were good, after all, but fights at home continued.

In the hills of Nagaland, meanwhile, my life unfurled. I worked hard, found and lost love, could not bring myself to get married, found women and children who guided me, sheltered me, gained my affection, and built for me the purposeful life that I hadn't planned.

Auntie and the kids

Smoked pork in *axone*, fresh pork in dried bamboo shoot, snails in *anishi*, frogs, fish, chicken or pork hooves in fresh bamboo shoot, *kholar*, boiled vegetables and leaves to go with chutneys that contain a smattering of several types of chillies, dried fish, tree tomato, ginger, beans, and so on. Auntie always claimed to be a poor cook but barring her partiality to salt, which we eventually controlled, she scooped up some fine food to quench the soul.

I found Auntie through an advertisement in the *Nagaland Post* in October 2012. At her rented apartment in Dimapur, she had a spot open for a 'working woman paying guest'. I had been scuttling across the Naga areas since 2011, and felt the need for a temporary-type permanent space in Dimapur that was flexible with its timings and rules to accommodate my life as a journalist.

Like many Naga women, Auntie—now a primary school teacher by profession—had spent years of her youth studying and working in New Delhi and understood the housing needs of working women. Her first child, Punarepla, was two at the time, clung to her mother, was annoyed at her showering attention on anyone else but her, and spoke plenty gibberish. We traded a deal—I could rent a whole room, all of three concrete walls and a half plywood partition, a shared bathroom, two meals a day, and a key each to the main gate and the house, to enter any time of the night. But I, and anyone else I brought home, including my parents, had to call her 'Auntie.' We lived together happily ever after.

In 2014, their second child, Sheratenla, was born. As the kids grew up, our family expanded to include a parrot, a rabbit, a cat and a dog. Every autumn, flying ants zoomed out of wall cavities; catching them to put into the dinner chutney became our family sport. We lived in an old Assam-type house in Dimapur, with a little yard that mostly hosted the animals and firewood that Auntie's husband chopped and brought from a friend's farm. This could be sold for some extra cash. It wasn't easy to bring up children in cities where avenues for earning were slim.

Auntie's husband is a prodigy. He never had the opportunity to complete higher education but had once attempted, in his adult life, to engineer a pair of wings to fly. When he 'flew' off the roof he thumped to the ground, breaking only an ankle. This was one of his only failures in engineering design. A master carpenter and electrician, he could dismantle a whole house and put it back together like a classic Lego puzzle. He could break down, assemble and recreate air guns, motors of any machine or vehicle, phones and computers. Yet people like him found it difficult to get a regular job in Nagaland. Alongside the quiet temperament of a scientist, he embodied many traits of a Naga patriarch. The rare jobs that friends, familiar with his work, offered, plus managing the constant repair work that our old and rotting house needed, kept him busy on most days.

In this practically single-woman-run household, Auntie earned, cleaned, cooked and nurtured her family and me. Her community was always around. Aunts, uncles, friends, clan members, village members, church members, the homeless, the drunks, the indebted, the sick, a nephew without parental support, a niece struggling to finish school, card-game addicts, domestic abuse victims, achievers, failures—everyone congregated under Auntie's roof with the comfort of her hospitality and the warmth of her love. If nothing else, a plate of rice or a cup of tea, or a bed and blanket, were always available for anyone willing or in need of them.

She knew I had no family or friends in Nagaland when I first came here, and she gave me the gift of both. The girls only know me as 'aheli,' no relational aspects are questioned; my room is plastered with drawings that grew up with them; some that we made together, others they made and hung up and arranged themselves. Punarepla helps me salvage my poor fashion sense; Sheratenla is preparing to watch her first movie in a theatre with her sister and me. Auntie checks my plate with every meal to ensure neighbours don't think I'm becoming too thin, while also satiating my socialised dietary needs.

Whenever I bring goodies from home that I try to hide and hoard just for myself, Auntie reveals her sweet tooth. Sharing doesn't cost much, she says, while reserving the stomach pieces of fish, one piece each for the girls and me; I hand over the *gur er shondesh* in return. The girls find my packed-from-home Bangali food 'stinky', but unlike some house owners in Delhi or Bangalore who deny people from the North East housing due to unfamiliarity with their food, these little girls look into my plate of strange items, make a face and move on. Auntie's care afforded me a contented life as a single woman journalist at *The Morung Express*. When I had a stomach ache, there was *tangmo* to relieve it. When stories failed, there was a fireplace and someone with a ready ear always loitering around it or mourning their own losses, to comfort or find comfort in. When battles were won there was a celebration brew. Her family and friends are also mine, to have a meal with or to go to Christmas carnivals and New Year picnics with. But over-familiarity breeds comfort. 'It is time for you to marry a Naga man,' say various family members. With families, blood-wise or otherwise, some things never change.

Single women of the Naga hills

Barring those with desk jobs in urban areas who struggle to keep their belly in and chest, arms and legs chiselled, Naga men are a fit lot. Even in an urban area, many cut firewood on a regular basis, build and repair their own homes, take care of children, butcher meat, clean up *hamok* (snail) shells and cook the snails, too.

Yet many Naga women, ten to fifteen years older than me, or my age, chose to remain single. Following decades of a struggle for political self-determination that was crushed brutally, albeit unsuccessfully, by the Indian state, many men of the previous generation took to drugs—if they hadn't already been killed by war. The Naga Mothers' Association (NMA), which included all Naga mothers as members, led a courageous battle against both militarisation and drug abuse. With the help of women who also took over the reins of managing families and households, men emerged and put the violently scattered pieces of their lives back together. But then came alcohol. A prohibition on alcohol in place in Nagaland since 1989, neither plugged the flow of spurious liquor into the market, nor the deaths due to liver damage. Almost every household hosted an alcoholic, or an alcoholic who beat the bottle with help from the Church and NMA. Many young men joined a Naga movement during the ceasefire, often left with no other option to earn a living, and found themselves in jail, trapped by India's National Security Act. Like Naga nationalist leaders living in an Indian government-provided residence in New Delhi, everyone was in a state of flux as the Indo-Naga Peace Process chugged up and down the tracks since the 1997 ceasefire. While many women did marry these uncommon characters of a no-war-no-peace society, many chose not to.

Naga women had silently borne a huge burden of the Indo-Naga conflict. Where men struggled to integrate socially into the new ceasefire society, women found themselves on the other side of the threshold. Before the conflict they had no rights to ancestral property and they do not have them now, after the ceasefire. They were not represented in village or elders' councils earlier, nor are they now. The sexual violence and humiliation heaped on them by the Indian Army—forced to give birth in jungles, in public or in concentration camps set up by the army, a trauma from which many mothers never recovered, and that they passed on to their children—had disturbed them immensely, but the women dutifully went back to their hearths, fields and jobs. They carried on.

In December 2011, I had an opportunity to work with a group of Naga women whose parents had been directly affected by the war and were now rebuilding their societies in the midst of the Indo-Naga Peace Process. They had helped set up the North East Network's Resource Centre in Chizami village of Phek district.

Years ago, Seno Tsühah had been reprimanded by an uncle for moving around *jhum* fields with a *dao*. Uncle was miffed by the *dao*-holder, held in place by a woven belt around the waist, in which she had tucked the *dao*. Seno was attempting to climb an alder tree to fetch mould from the tree's hollow to use for her kitchen garden. Without the handy bamboo *dao*-holder (supposed to be worn only by men) it was difficult to climb the tree, and risky if one were to fall. So Seno did what was practical then and each time afterwards. She carried the *dao* in the belt designed to carry it safely. Another time, she wore camouflage canvas hunting boots to an expedition to collect jungle leaves 'because they have the best grip'. A group of women who saw her could not control their laughter. Hunting boots were worn only by men at the time, women had to make do with sandals even as they carried heavy firewood up and down the hills. Eventually, some of these women followed Seno's example to become leaders in their communities, challenging taboos, norms and oppressive structures.

With her mind firmly in place, Seno chose to remain single. She is considered a leader among indigenous communities worldwide, representing their voices in international forums. She and her team worked on issues of farming, weaving, women's rights, indigenous seed banks, reproductive rights, ecology, climate change and more with her village, with those in the neighbourhood, and eventually, with remote villages in Eastern Nagaland, recognising and honouring the scientific work of seed preservation that women in these villages were doing, inadvertently leading their societies towards a holistic future. In recognition of the lives she transformed in Chizami and elsewhere, village elders and the community donated land to their team to set up a resource centre. The women who work here, mostly from the village or surrounding villages, many of them single, not only know their Foxtail millets from Pearl and Proso, they can cook them in ten different ways, fetch firewood, cut it, identify an innumerable array of wild and tamed consumable and medicinal leaves, butcher meat, make a fire, cook a community feast, teach, weave, garden, travel to unknown places, write grants, execute projects, make decisions for the community, make beds and always tuck their guests in with a fantastic story! On icy cold mornings, they are awake before anyone else, preparing for the day with a piping hot cup of tea.

Today, women comfortably wear hunting boots, and a woman representative sits at Chizami, as well as its neighbouring Sümi, and in village council meetings, taking part in formulating public policy. The Chizami Baptist Church has elected a young single woman as its pastor, a rare feat for Naga Baptist churches.

Although single women in the Naga hills have no right to inherit ancestral property, in some villages they can use ancestral land during their lifetime. They have marginal voices in family or clan and village meetings. Without a husband or child to claim social legitimacy, the choice to remain single here is hard—behind their backs, single women are often made fun of: is she cursed? Yet, the choice is becoming easier for women who want to, or can, study, work, earn enough to buy their own property if they want to, and live in any way they desire, within the limits of what their society will allow.

They are using their time to make their communities more progressive, easing the collective pain of shuttling into a new market economy. In one remote eastern district, a single woman hammered accountability into the district's public healthcare system, and set up a school for the underprivileged in a farther unconnected region. In Dimapur, a Naga filmmaker, a single woman, made a film about the transgender community in Nagaland for the first time, despite the criticism she knew she was bound to face in a society that rejects multiple sexual identities. There are single women who are doing the 'will of God' and that of the Nagaland Baptist Church Council, serving as missionaries in various states in India and across the world, particularly in the difficult mission fields of Africa and China. There are women, single by choice, serving in the various Naga armies, waiting for Naga self-determination to become a reality.

The only worry, as all of us are asked, is how will we manage when we grow old?

'We still have a close-knit family and cohesive community here, so it is not such a big problem to be single and old,' says Seno. But many young people are leaving the villages and social dimensions are shifting. 'We could also opt to live in an old age home,' she shrugs, though such support systems are not easily accessible or affordable. Her point is that love and care are not limited to biological families or restricted to marital institutions; they can be found in a sharing circle of friends or among other people in new communities, too.

With the inspiring work she is already doing, in turn inspiring women like us to remain confident in our singledom, this is a long-term worry. But unlike women like me, who do not live with our immediate families, Naga women are lifelong caregivers, tending to parents, siblings, nephews and nieces.

All in all, I am in good company. Life's much smoother with an endless afternoon at the end of the week, to learn from a photographer who is transforming the way Dimapur, and Naga people's experience in it, is viewed. It helps that she is a single woman, too. Life is smoother still on the rugged roads to be traversed without the sound of a phone call and text message, no child back home to worry about, where work is joyous, with no holds on the kind of stories covered, and fewer boundaries defining the person I am or will be. I am not a political or entertainment journalist—I cover anything and everything that unfurls locally, giving credence to all human experience, social, political, economic, psychological. The absence of boundaries in my life also defines (pushes?) the professional way forward.

Living far from home has other perks; especially if it is a place far enough away, where, according to my mother, no 'mainland' man in his right mind would move, even if he agreed to move at all for the sake of a wife's career. But then, I refused to move, too, for the sake of a love I once found in the remote hills, at the cost of the work I do with *The Morung Express*. Many older women, in Mumbai and in Nagaland, assume that it must be a man who keeps me in Nagaland. Thankfully not. Nobody has initiated an organised hunt to make this happen either—my parents are too conservative to look for a groom on the peripheries, and most communities here do not want to set their sons, brothers, nephews up with an 'outsider'. That lodges me in the mysterious *terra nullis*, leaving me, in essence, free.

After spending years trying to dislodge me from Nagaland, my parents have finally seen the value of the work that we at *The Morung Express*, shouldered by a bunch of single women, do. Here, I am freed of the burden to HAVE to be married, to hoard wealth, to move up the class ladder, to be defined by a man and his choice of ambition. I can choose to be defined by the journalism we do at *The Morung Express*, guided by the historical realities, voices and experiences of the Naga people. If marital pressure ever rears its head, there's always a PhD to pursue in a land far away.

All this doesn't stop me from falling in love, of course, and love is most exciting when the end of the tunnel is invisible, perhaps not even there. We find ways to see the light. My Bangali family has reconciled to that; hopefully my Naga family will, too.

Being single

SUJATA PATEL

I WAS SITTING IN THE SECOND CLASS COMPARTMENT OF THE Konarak Express heading to Bhubaneshwar. After a few hours of travel, the matriarch of the Marwari family sitting opposite me, about 60 years old (she had three generations with her), whose delectable lunch and snacks I had just eaten with great relish, asked me first my age (I must have been around 30 or 32 at the time), and after nodding wisely many times, asked, 'When did you get married and where is your husband?' Immediately thereafter followed another question: 'How many children do you have and who is looking after them?'

This was the first time I had been asked these questions and I was at a loss for words. After a few minutes of dilemma, I thought it best to be honest, and said with some nonchalance (buffered by a smile) that I did not have children or a husband and so was not married. Immediately her face showed signs of uneasiness, and with great concern she advised me to marry soon for, 'After all, who will do your shraddha?' At that moment I realised that the two of us, in spite of our bonding over food and small talk, were located in two different worlds and that there was an all-embracing social, intellectual and political distance between us. At the time, I did not have the requisite social or intellectual resources to communicate my point of view, and was flummoxed about how and in what manner to explain that being married or having a husband and children were not important issues for me, and that I did not need to explain this to anyone.

I was on my way to do fieldwork in the villages of Balasore district, Odisha. Over the course of the next month and a half, I was constantly asked the same question in the field: who was my husband and where was he? Over time, I found the requisite answer, which helped my respondents who were married and had families to understand me and, most importantly, accept me, so that I could continue with my research. I realised that it was best to say that I was educating myself and had very little time for other things. This was an answer that I came up with in the first few days, which became my refrain whenever this issue arose. It allowed me the space to not explain my choices and thereby maintain my privacy. By then, the mid-80s, even in the rural areas of Odisha, it was accepted that education and studying were important commitments (although only for males), and I remember how, in one household, as I gave this standard answer, a young girl of about 16 looked at me shyly and longingly, and stated, 'Only daughters of rich parents staying in towns have this choice.' Looking back, it was unfortunate that I did not take her aside to talk to her and find out how I could help her; post-facto, I regret that I did not do what I should have—comprehend her urge and help her realise it.

In 2005-06, a brilliant student of mine, a priest asked me: 'Is sociology your calling?' When I did not understand the import of his question he qualified it by asking, 'Is this why you are single?' and I realised that there is something here that needs consideration. At the time he was reflecting on the many complications affecting priesthood, and I wondered whether this question was asked because he thought that for priesthood, he needed to be single like I was, that this is what being committed to the profession entails! It is this conversation with my student that I recall as I write this essay and I wonder: why is it that being single is thought to be so unusual, and why is it a choice that questions the system? Why is it seen to be a decision that lets us take the first steps to achievement and empowerment, and is therefore a dangerous act for a girl? Why does this feat need a specific explanation and, depending on one's ideology and subject-position, generate positive or negative feelings and emotions, whereas being married is thought to be natural?

Unfortunately, since then I have not given myself time to think through this issue, and so I am glad that the opportunity has arisen now. For many years I thought I did not need to explain my choice of being single, that it is a very private matter. Today, as I write this, I think differently; that this choice is a political intervention and needs some analysis by activists and scholars, and that as a scholar I should map some of its contours.

I don't know if anyone *chooses* to remain single; circumstances make them exercise this choice at a certain point of time. In my case, I decided quite early in life that if I wished to nurture a child, I would adopt one; that before marrying, I needed to be employed; and that the first need not follow the second. Coincidently, after finding a job, my then relationship did not work out, so I started living alone and continued thus, because by then I was clear that this is the only way I can remain autonomous and unfettered from 'doing things' with one person all the time—maybe for my whole life. I also realised that I would like to use my energy to establish myself in my work/profession (always such a struggle for a woman of any class/caste) rather than deploying it to first comprehend, and later deliberate and negotiate differences in living and 'being' with a partner. I loved being alone and managing my own household and over time I became an accomplished homemaker. And so, after some years, getting married was no longer a choice. However, I need to add a caveat; though I lived alone in a rented home for a decade after I made this decision, my parents shifted into my household when they became infirm and needed care, and lived with me for almost fifteen years before they passed away in 2002 and 2013, respectively. Those were interesting times; on the one hand I learnt what caring was and on the other, I was exhausted by the caring and anguished by the slow decay in their physical and mental abilities. Since then, I have again started living alone and have appreciated and applauded the freedom and autonomy that I now have to live in the way I wish to.

For a woman to take a decision to be single demands that she be economically independent; receive acceptance and legitimacy for being single from her family and professional networks; own or make enough money to rent accommodation (generally difficult for single women who are not enmeshed in recognised family or kin networks); and has the strength to confront and sustain herself against the prejudice, discrimination and sexism heaped on her by all and sundry, of both sexes. Given that she does not carry the visible symbols (sindhur and/or mangalsutra) that protect her from patriarchal interrogation, she faces constant questions regarding her personal life from all manner of individuals, including from those who provide everyday services such as plumbers, electricians, telephone repairers, dhobis and domestic workers, to professional colleagues.

She also faces discrimination and/or pity at work, as most institutions in the public domain (whether headed by males or females) are misogynous. Males at work/professional sites do not know how to relate to single women as colleagues. (I recall when I was in hospital and very seriously ill, my male professional colleagues at Pune University sent their wives to enquire about my health rather than come themselves.) Some think single women are aggressive (women's assertiveness is perceived as aggression), hysterical, unaccommodating (because marriage would have tamed women to patriarchal principles) and too demanding, constantly questioning everyday practices, not knowing how to demonstrate obeisance to those in authority; standing up for their rights and those of others. All such ideas and impressions allow them to develop negative feelings for single women. Such men and women gossip about them, think that single women, being sexually unfulfilled, are ready for one-night stands or affairs. Thus, a single woman has to confront predators of all kinds, not only those who create obstacles to her advancement in institutions/professions but also those who prey on her body. These colleagues (both male and female) can use their power and authority within the official structures to question the single woman's everyday alternate professional practices, especially if they feel threatened by her constant assertion for hers and others' independence and autonomy. I am sure that, like me, many single women (more than married ones) have faced both inquisitions and formal inquiries because of their insistence on being self-assertive.

Single women need to sustain themselves by creating alternate support structures and new networks of friendship. However creating these is difficult, if not impossible, given that most individuals network and build relationships as couples, with or without children, and operate within accepted class-based kin and caste groups. Being single is not easy; it is a major struggle and does not come without initiating all manner of battles to maintain material and psychological autonomy and freedom. Most of the time, women who are single also support their parents and/or siblings. It is extremely difficult for a woman from a low income background to make this choice; they are married very early in life even before they can understand their agency in order to take such a decision.

In these circumstances, I take the statistics made popular by the Government of India's Ministry of Women and Child Welfare, that there are about 71 million single women in India (an increase of almost 39 per cent from the 2001 Census) with a pinch of salt. These women are single because they may be widowed, separated and/or divorced or deserted by their husbands and/or children, and his family, also oftentimes discarded by their natal families. Demographers have informed us that most women in India are married by the time they are 19, and almost 99 per cent are married by the time they are 30. The above statistics on singleness relate to those who have become single *after marriage*. Such single women face enormous difficulties and vulnerabilities; material, social and psychological, together with sexual harassment, prejudice and discrimination. But one needs to distinguish this single-ness from the one that we are discussing in this book.

I am now convinced that being single, that is, being never-married, is a state that questions the way the institutions of marriage-family-kin organise the private domain and intersect with the public domain in India. The choice to remain single not only subverts these institutions and norms of behaviour that ensure women's subordination, but affirms her agency to constitute a distinctive and alternative lifestyle. This empowers her to interrogate the private-public institutions that had earlier entangled her into accepting and legitimising her dependent personality, and reproduce her identity within the cultural site of 'home production'.[1] It also allows her to question the power that such institutions have over her labour/work, friendship networks and social capital; and over sexual choices. It enables her to situate her emotions of love, happiness and joy, as also of hurt, anger and disgust, on a completely different and new register than the one that has, thus far, organised emotions for married women.

This act of subversion gives her a new agency which she is sometimes conscious of, sometimes not. For women who become aware of the agency, being single provides them with further intellectual resources to extend the critique of domination and power that they have developed as a consequence of single-ness and extend it to other institutions within the public domain. It enables them to play a public role in analysing the way symbolic and cultural power finds its expression in the public domain, and to question ways in which everyday overt and covert violence stamps our public arenas. Ultimately, single-ness provides one with intellectual resources to comprehend the true meaning of difference, individuation, equality and democracy.

Being single, therefore, finds expression in various ways, sometimes as defiance, at other times in symbolic silence, and at still others, in protest. It promotes an attitude of fearlessness and pluckiness, and encourages daring, courage and bravery to struggle against all odds. It also asserts the woman as an independent persona, an autonomous, sovereign, self-sufficient and free individual in control of her body, emotions, feelings and ideas. Single-ness, I think, means all this and more. This essay explores my family background and its imperatives, and combines analysis with my personal journey to comprehend what it means to be a single woman, for me.

I grew up as an only child, born when my parents were in their middle years: 35 and 41. By then they had been married for almost two decades and were immersed in themselves, their work and their public/political commitments. They were also working parents—they would leave home at 7.30-8.00 a.m. and return at

6.00-7.00 p.m., sometimes even later. My only interaction with them was generally late on Saturdays (when they had half-day work) and on Sundays.

I recall, as I was growing up, listening to their concerns and their interventions on issues concerning the experimental school that they were managing as principal and teacher, respectively. I think I unconsciously assimilated their thoughts on education, pedagogy, learning, and particularly, on Gandhi's views on education, about Gandhians and their experiments in ashram-schools and other such institutions. I also learnt about their own involvement in many other public activities in Mumbai and Gujarat and the rest of the country. I grew into adulthood early, concerned with ideas governing the public domain of the country, and had little or no time for games or my peers.

Not all single children of middle-aged parents involved with radical public concerns grow up to be single. But my childhood experience set the pattern for my living alone. My socialisation as a single child allowed me to learn to embrace a feeling of aloneness, of being with myself, with my books and my daydreams. I recall loving the solitude and silence that surrounded me, and I still love it. I didn't think that being alone was strange; felt that this was the only way to be. It also made me feel that I have to learn to depend on myself for everything and be self-sufficient, and led me to learn to live with, and create a world for, myself.

This silence and the notion of privacy that I constructed around myself was reinforced because our family had little or no interaction with my parents' extended family and kin group. My parents had eloped and got married when they were 16 and 21, respectively, and had practically no contact in the early years of married life with either of their natal families. Immediately after their marriage, they got involved with the national movement and forged deep bonds with their compatriots from the Congress party and other radical groups, including communists. And although by the time I was born, contact had been established with my mother's sister and her family, and later with my father's family, I grew up without having any clear understanding of the enmeshed relationships of blood that organise intimate interactions within kin/caste groups. To me, my family was my mother's friends, whether young or old, whom I sometimes called masi(s) and masa(s), but more often by their first names.

A chance remark by the social historian, Ravinder Kumar, about Gandhi and how he created an alternate political family/ kin group, bonding young and old, women and men, ashram-ites and party workers on public and private concerns, through his letters, made me understand the origin of my own family network. I realised that by creating a friendship network that bonded over public concerns, my parents and their friends were also creating an alternate family/kin group, based on non-blood relationships. Additionally, I was never asked whether I wanted to get married—I guess my parents would have found it difficult to find someone for me, given that they and their various friends took their own decisions on this issue. The only prescription that I remember being given is that I needed to study, and get a reasonably good job. I was also encouraged to become economically independent very early; my higher education abroad and in India was mostly covered through awards and fellowships.

One of the lessons I learnt in my early years, which has resonated in many of my personal decisions (including being single) and which has imprinted my scholarship, relates to an assessment of power and its entanglement in personal lives. Though never discussed upfront, I grew up with the notion that one must move away from the lure of power/authority to ensure freedom and autonomy for oneself. I learnt to be wary of power of all kinds: interpersonal, institutional and that of ideas. This principle found its significance in daily practices within the family. I was brought up to have few needs, live a life of simplicity, invest only in functional commodities and to recycle everything that I possessed. I recall rebelling against some of these strictures, especially after seeing my peers with new clothes or finding my own favourite clothes and books being recycled to others. Over time I appreciated the importance of this principle, in addition to its being embedded in ecological wisdom.

I also learnt very early how the lure of power can displace one's commitments, an understanding that has remained ever-present in my consciousness and has affected my everyday life and choices. The first lesson I learnt about this concerns my mother. My mother was an important member of the Congress party. She was in jail, first at Arthur Road and then at Yeravda, for more than a year during the Quit India movement, and after that achieved a high position within the hierarchy of the Bombay Pradesh Congress Committee. After learning about Gandhi's call to all Congress workers to resign, she immediately left the party. She was offered all kinds of enticements, including a promise of a parliamentary seat in the 1952 elections, if she maintained her membership. But she remained steadfast in her resolve. Soon after resigning, she followed Gandhi's advice to get involved in social/constructive activities, and later associated herself with my father in the educational experiments he had initiated while implementing Gandhian basic education practices in schools. It must have taken a lot of courage for her to give up the power she had achieved within the party, which would have allowed her to walk into the public domain and obtain nation-wide recognition and fame.

The second was an incident related to my father. We received intimation that he had been given an award for the work he had done in school education, and that he should go immediately to Delhi to receive it from the President. I recall my mother's excitement, and then her extreme disappointment when he refused to accept it because it was given to him by the government/ state—he did not want his autonomy and possible future critical interventions against the Indian state to be compromised by accepting the award.

From this I realised that my father believed that if one covets power, it distorts one's moral compass. My mother also upheld this principle. I learnt unconsciously that one should not make oneself subservient to an individual/parent/guru or a collectivity; to an idol or to a religion; to institutions, group solidarities or political parties and their ideologies. Some of these ideas were an interpretation of Gandhian positions, but they also carried with them other traces, of Rabindranath Tagore's ideas on education, and of the merit in recognising difference and its implications for democracy, as advocated by the philosopher John Dewey, whose views had influenced my father when he was at Columbia University. No wonder there were no photographs (including those of us, the family) or statues and paintings of gods or individuals (including Gandhi) in our home.

Another incident that remains imprinted relates to the months just before the Emergency was declared in 1975. I had bought, and hung on the wall just above the dining table, a lithograph of Karl Marx made by Vivan Sundaram. The same evening my father held a meeting of the Akhil Bharatiya Nai Talim Samiti at our home, as secretary of the organisation. One of his colleagues teased him about this lithograph, but he did not take the bait and explained it away as a sketch of his grandfather! I realised then how much he appreciated my right to be different from him, both personally and politically, and to uphold this right, he was willing to leave the lithograph on the wall and suspend his own (strong) views against Marx, as well as of making gurus of individuals.

This principle dominated everyday practices in the family. Each of us started the day with different drinks: coffee for my father, tea for my mother, and lemon and honey water for me. Though my parents only wore khadi, I was asked to make my own choices. But more significant was the lesson I learnt from my parents' marriage and their relationship with each other. I was just 13 or 14 years old when I became conscious of the differences in my parents' personalities, expectations and needs. I also started noting arguments and raised voices (mainly my mother's) between them. One day, when my father and I were sitting and reading the newspapers, my mother walked into the room and said that she was leaving us. She had a suitcase with her. I recall feeling shocked and had tears flowing down my face.

My father did not say a word and gestured to me to stop crying. I later realised that he did this so that my mother would not feel pressurised to change her mind about her decision. He merely asked her whether he should get her a taxi. She declined, and left. Today I can't recall when she came back, except that one day, returning from school, I noticed that her clothes were back and that she had gone to work.

Her coming back had an impact on my life. I noticed that I was encouraged to make friends and organise activities on my own, and my involvement with my parents' activities decreased. After I completed my schooling at 16, I was almost pushed out of home and encouraged to make friends of my own and travel outside Bombay, as much as possible. As a consequence I was able to carve out my own identity, be recognised for myself and was no longer known only for my relationship with my parents. Later, many individuals were astonished to learn who my parents were; we were so different in all aspects: politics and ideology, lifestyle and personal choices.

But if this event sowed within me the first doubt regarding marriage as an institution, it also made me conscious that even a perfect relationship (which was what I thought my parents had), changes and becomes not-so-perfect as new needs and expectations arise between two closely intertwined yet strong-willed individuals, one of whom was passionately committed to his ideas. Years later, I wondered whether the break happened because my mother could not find her space and her identity. She was too young when she married, and if she had continued in politics, she might have forged a new life and become a different person.

Growing up with such freedoms was a challenge, but it made me develop skills not only to comprehend myself, my needs and expectations, but also to understand those of other people, whether young or old, female or male. It also made me self-conscious and observant, learn ways to establish intimacies and trust, and simultaneously cultivate bonds of care, nurture and sexual companionship across wide networks. Through them I learnt to organise my emotional commitments. I grew up to think that such families were normal, and drew my emotional strength and even material support from this 'institution'. I believe that my family is constituted of people whose age and sex, size and numbers were, and are, always changing. It includes friends of my parents (who are alive), their children, and my own friends of long years, made during my travels. It has been expanded today to include some of my ex-students.

My being single has a lot to do with being a 'traveller'. I was initiated into taking journeys by my parents. They were always travelling for meetings, work and other activities, and took me along. I think I must have seen the entire country at least three or four times, visiting both historical/religious and tourist sites during school vacations, including doing the Badri-Kedar treks and understanding these sites variously for their ecological/environmental/aesthetic value, as well as for their modern and contemporary significance and their importance in nation-building. It was on these travels that I learnt what diversity is and the need to reject all kinds of religiosity and insularity.

After the age of 16, I was encouraged to go on these journeys with a friend or even alone. Inevitably we travelled in second class compartments and lived cheaply, sometimes in low-priced hotels/dharamshalas, and consumed whatever was available on stations or dhabas. I recall once taking a five-hour journey in Bihar on the steps of a railway compartment, as my reserved seat had been occupied by a gang of young men. Travelling alone challenged me to be courageous and tough. Not only did I learn the geography, history and culture of India (and later of the world) but also simple things such as how and where to buy bus and train tickets, how to negotiate fines when travelling ticketless; find food; trek in unknown mountainous regions; convince lorry drivers to drop me/us at the nearest town while warding off their sexist behaviour. I learnt how to take risks, make mistakes and emerge resilient and strong from these experiences. In fact, I realised slowly that to learn something new I need to travel, and that taking a journey should become my way of life/being; being on the move became important, both physically and metaphorically.

From the late 1970s, my travels took on a new orientation. The trigger for this was a letter I received from my mother some time in September 1975, after I reached Canada where I went to complete a master's degree. I left India in late July 1975, a few weeks after the Emergency was declared in India. In that letter, my mother narrated all the events that had taken place after the imposition of the Emergency, and wrote how personally traumatic it was for her not to participate in the demonstrations that began soon after June 26. She decided against participating in them as she knew that in case she was arrested, I might decide not to go to Canada for further studies, and that I might also participate in the demonstrations—by then I had started taking an interest in the nascent civil/democratic rights movement being organised in the city. This letter haunted me during my 14-15 month stay in Canada and on my travels across North America and Europe during the summer of that year. When I completed my master's degree I returned to India, and realised immediately that I could not remain an outsider, surveying social and political developments affecting the country; I needed to become an insider and, through this process, find meaning for my person, myself and my life.

Within a few months of my return the Emergency was lifted. I met those who had been released from prison and reconnected with friends who were involved in civil/democratic rights movements. For the next decade, till the end of the 1990s, I remained active in the Committee for Democratic Rights (CDR) and later, when I registered for a doctorate at Jawaharlal Nehru University in Delhi, with the Peoples' Union for Democratic Rights (PUDR). This was when we saw the growth of protest movements across the country. Over the decade, as I did field-work, first as a doctoral student and later as an independent research scholar studying contemporary social movements, I connected with social and political activists who had become involved in public concerns and in various social movements across the country, who subsequently became, and remain, my friends even today.

As I travelled on foot, in processions, in buses, trucks and boats with the populace and activists who wanted to question state power, I perceived how these political concerns are significant to grasp contemporary issues concerning the country. But I also realised how the women involved in these movements were rarely acknowledged by male leaders. (who could be members of their families/kin-caste/tribal groups) while some others had faced sexist onslaughts. This led me to understand how power plays out within social movements and how male/patriarchal power interlaces the public and private domains at many levels, from everyday lives to in/formal institutions, from parties or NGOs to the state. I heard the narratives of women activists as they discussed their struggles to find their space and their identity within the movement, and within the household, about the sexism, abuse, violence and rape suffered by some of them, both within the home and outside it. And I felt a surge of hope as I listened to various activists in the autonomous women's movement wishing to question, disrupt and dislocate patriarchal power. Things *will* change.

Over the years, I have tried to comprehend the moorings of sexist and misogynous cultures in the intersecting 'secular' private-public domains of our country. While I could understand (but not accept) how blood-based caste-kin relations fostered such misogyny, I was astounded to see that these could also be reproduced in the families of 'progressive' couples within academia and activism. I learnt that such families need not be different from those organised through arranged marriages. Both these promote sexist partnerships in which there is a strict sexual division of labour, wherein the male is the dominant figure and his professional and emotional needs and expectations organise the household. More often than not wives/partners cooked and looked after the home, and after bearing children nurtured them to become employable adults. When husbands could not find permanent jobs, wives worked to manage the household. While some of these wives/partners forgot about their own ambitions, husbands stayed at home, did some consultancies, read, reflected and held forth on their academic/political work, while the wives listened, encouraged and propped up their egos. I don't think these husbands or their children ever thought it important to understand their wives' or mothers' desires. Nor did they worry about how they were coping with double and treble workloads. If any of these women were able to manage their professional and personal lives, it was because they could afford domestic help to look after their households.

I found that these marriages/partnerships were oriented towards achieving the ambitions of the male partner, whether in the profession or in alternate politics, and together the couple reproduced a family strategy to command the status for the family in many differing ways. Such couples rarely lived as two individuals investing in reproducing a household/family that respected differences, shared household work, jointly nurtured their children and made space for all of them to grow differently. Surely reproducing a democratic and inclusive family is also a political project?

This scenario anguished and disturbed me and I asked myself why marriages between so-called progressives repeat conservative patterns? Does wanting a child and a family necessarily imply being in an unequal relationship? Does the fear of living alone imply that one must live with such compromises?

I am convinced today that we need to interrogate unequal practices in the private domain. These reproduce and legitimise male ambitions to triumph in the public domain, and accept their competitiveness as the basis for reconstituting utopias of change within scholarship/politics. Without this, there will be little questioning of clientism, patronage and instrumental wheeling-dealing that govern our public domain, whether by the mainstream or the radical elite. The absence allows 'progressive' males and females to sidestep and, more often, to fudge or make opaque, practices related to class/caste/patriarchy patronage within professional/activist cultures. The inequity of practices within the household has promoted the reproduction of patriarchal and misogynous cultures in the public domain. In turn, given that males overwhelmingly dominate authority positions in the public domain these patriarchies legitimise class/caste based masculinities. Thus, misogynous practices are produced and reproduced in intersecting public-personal relationships. I have been intrigued by the fact that, in spite of the recognition of such private-public intersecting misogynous cultures, feminists continue to produce texts that discuss how to improve, and make equal, practices within marriage and family systems, rather than examine the way institutions are subverting these mainstream systems.

After I joined the teaching profession I have tried to communicate in my classrooms how marriage represents deep-seated power relationships. I have argued that marriage camouflages three desires which can be realised without the act of being married: sex/lust, reproduction/children, and companionship. Individuals may not want to realise all three at any one stage of one's life cycle. However, given the overwhelming power of this institution in everyday cultural practice and in the media, it has been difficult to convince young women of this position. One of the reasons why we don't understand that marriage is unnecessary is because of the normative value placed on biological reproduction. It is thus important that, as a first step, we move away from the official understanding of the joint/extended heterosexual family sharing one residence/household, enmeshed in blood relationships organised through kin and caste groups, and try to explore how groups live together without such rules or norms.

I have found many examples of alternative ways of living together in common residences or households of fe/male groups that have no blood relationship with each other. While some of them are formed for ideological reasons (such as communes for political, religious and recently, ecological reasons) others are organised around survival. The latter is particularly true in poor countries like India. I am not suggesting that these formations do not reproduce new hierarchies and are not enmeshed in dominant-subordinate relationships. However, recognising these forms is important as it will help to puncture the notion that common residences are only possible through kin-based marriage. For example, many of us growing up in middle class buildings in south Bombay have encountered families or households formed by male working class domestics, who cook, eat and live in small one-room tenements, called *kholis*, for decades until they retire from domestic work. It is unfortunate that we are not documenting and recording these alternate family-household networks that continue to sustain unorganised informal work in India.

Years later, when one very sensitive and adventurous student wanted to write a dissertation on conflicts and tensions in Indian family life, I convinced her to direct her gaze outside the ideal type of family popularised as a norm by the Indian middle classes. I asked her to focus instead on networks of support, care, nurturance, and material and emotional sustenance made by runaway kids at railway stations, the latter becoming their place of residence and cohabitation. This helped me to understand how new forms of trust were being constituted even among children or young people of both sexes. It affirmed how the urge for human connection transcends age, and allowed me to see how non-blood families or households were being built in contemporary India, where precarity determines the long-term family and household life of the poor.

We need to live together and develop trust among ourselves because we are sociable beings. Can we not make families of single individuals from different age groups?

Notes

My sincere thanks to Aban, Anu, Lakshmi, Navaz, Pooja, Prachi, Sonalben and Vishal, who read and commented on this paper. Errors if any are mine

1 Women are trained or socialised to produce and reproduce the home. Their labour is deployed to enhance the status and mobility of the family as a whole. This consists of a basket of tasks and roles, including income generation, but also childcare, housework, networking with extended kin and community, meeting obligations, nurturing relationships, as well as preserving cultural notions of honour and prestige. Hannah Papanek has called it 'status production' while other scholars have called it 'home production'.

Freak singlehood vows

embarking upon singlehood early,
with purpose and deliberation

SHARANYA GOPINATHAN

GROWING UP, MARRIAGE WASN'T REALLY SOMETHING MY parents and I talked much about. I sometimes wish I had broached the subject earlier and gradually, because I'm not sure they know exactly where I stand right now, so utterly convinced and full of 26-year-old certainty that I am. You see, growing up I was always the psychedelic freak sheep of my family, and I'm pretty sure that at some point my mother actually began wishing my teenage rebellion had more to do with boys than with marijuana. Amidst all that, we found no real reason to have the more uncomfortable discussions about men and marriage.

My older sister married her boyfriend and the big love of her life at 23, but I was always The Younger One, so the laws of time and consequence broke and bent and crashed around me. I was perpetually considered too young for everything, even when I wasn't. So for years, I've been able to successfully leap around their jokes and faux-innocent repetitions of what other relatives had suggested about my marriage with my deliberately youthful joking, laughing the idea off as if it were hilarious, and then basically running away quickly.

But now I wish I had spoken to them straight instead of upending this bomb on them, as I will soon have to. You see, my parents have a completely different worldview than I do. All their nieces were married by 26, many well before they were 22. While my parents understand that this will not be happening in my case, enthusiastically support me in my writing and other bizarre endeavours, and certainly don't put any pressure on me to marry right away, I do think they harbour the belief that I will eventually marry. I have not told them that this is not at all how I plan to live. And now I think the time has come for me to just gird my loins and get it over with, to needlessly break my mother's heart and tell her I'm going to be #forever alone.

The romance novels I stole from my sister when I was 13, most of which were by the really rather remarkable American author, Nora Roberts, subconsciously informed the way I thought about the ideal romance through most of my teenage life. In these books, events inevitably followed a very specific trajectory. The young, heterosexual women were all progressive and 'modern', and their 'ballsiness' (an ironic term to use for cool women, but unfortunately every feminine equivalent simply sounds contrived) was elucidated very explicitly early on in the story. These women were all tough or artsy entrepreneurs, or had successful careers based on the natural gifts they were born with (plus one social worker, a deep sea diver and an art curator). They all met The One, fought bitterly against falling in love because they were too independent and wary and suspicious of smooth men, but after either catching an evil criminal or resolving an old family or childhood conflict, they would, upon some charming persuasion, finally agree to be married. The *End*.

This particular sequence of events, this idea of modern women, their modern routes to inevitable marriage, and the consequent total and absolute End of Their Story, infused my understanding of life quite thoroughly when I was younger. Given that I absorbed it as early as I did, it sort of trickled through my brain and settled down into the rest of the accumulated mental sediment I unconsciously carried around, mingling with other amorphous, unquestioningly-held beliefs, like: I must make lots of money, it doesn't matter how, purely because it was imperative that I become an independent woman, never at the *financial* mercy of any man in the world. This understanding also made it rather hard to see beyond my life at 29, deliriously in love with and happily married to a sexy, dangerously handsome man.

What I am trying to say is that for a very long time, I never stopped to question my own assumption that I would be married some day. It's what the books, the movies and the lives of all my relatives told me. Ideally, I imagined, I would have a job and choose my own husband, and these two factors would combine to mean that I was a highly empowered woman.

Breaking out of the arranged marriage system—as individuals, I mean, not as castes or communities—seemed to be the immediate preoccupation of my peers and myself in our teens. We did not want to marry the BITS Pilani boy from our caste-communities that our parents selected for us: we wanted to marry boys we selected for ourselves, from any state or community (but almost inevitably, from analogous castes and classes). We wanted to decide for ourselves when we married them, and to make sure that we had jobs before we did. We did not stop to think about whether we wanted to be married at all, because that was some kind of foregone conclusion. We just wanted to wear mirrored sunglasses on our wedding days, and to have the whole party documented by artsy candid portrait photographers, instead of staged line-ups shot by four moustachioed men. For a while at least, we did not really explore breaking out of the inherently restrictive, regressive, and casteist (did you know only somewhere between 5 and 12 per cent of marriages in India are inter-caste?) structure of marriage itself.

As poet and author, Sharanya Manivannan says, 'If, after all your relationships, your flings and pretensions, you still end up marrying someone from your caste, it says a lot about how problematic the institution of marriage is.'

As aware as I am of the casteist significance of marriage as an institution, I must admit that this was unfortunately not the factor that personally made me choose never to enter it. Rather, it was slowly coming to the realisation that marriage, such as it is, just doesn't *work* anymore.

It's difficult for me to imagine that I won't change in the next ten years. I feel like I have grown so much even in the last two, in ways that I possibly couldn't even fathom then, because I hadn't gone through the range of experiences I needed to learn and grow as I did. It seems ludicrous to me to imagine that I will be able to choose, at any given point of time, the single person I want to spend all my hours with for the rest of my life. I think I can find three broad reasons for this, two quite general, one perhaps slightly more specific to me.

The first, of course, is that it's hard enough to grow and change on your own, and to make adjustments to life and new environments and experiences. How on earth, really, can I expect anyone else to grow and change on exactly the same trajectory as I have, and how can I or anyone imagine that the person I will be in each decade will correspond to, or connect even vaguely with, this person I supposedly chose forever at age 23?

It just feels like a lot of pressure to put on myself and someone else. We enter marriages expecting to love and be loved, and not being able to experience either or both at any point does irreparable damage not just to our emotional selves, but also to the marriage itself. You need to be deeply in love with someone to stomach living with them, to even have a shot at being attracted to them all the time, and the moments when you don't feel that way lend themselves too easily to thinking deeply uncharitable, damaging thoughts about your partner. They also make it harder to pick yourself or your relationship up later.

I think I would also be the sort of person who, if informed that I was now married to someone, would measure up every tiny annoying thing they did and then say to myself, 'Oh my god! Am I going to have to deal with this for the *rest of my life*?' It feels like putting undue pressure on what could otherwise be a fairly nice relationship, and a surefire way to ensure that it ends, and ends quite resentfully at that.

The other thing is, and this might be localised a bit more to me, I don't really want to spend that much time with *any*one, and living together feels like an almost-compulsory feature of marriage. I'm the kind of person who needs to be alone for very long periods in order to feel okay, and I also adjust myself constantly depending on my company. Being on my own is what allows my soul and my personality to rest and recharge, and I don't consider this a bad thing; it's just the way I am. Now that I know this about myself, why would I want someone constantly in my house, never giving me the time and space I need to let my soul relax completely? I am only truly ever myself when I'm completely alone, and I don't want to deprive myself of that for anyone.

More broadly though, and most important of all, I think marriage as we know it was created for a time that looked nothing like the one we live in today. Every major religion assigns very specific roles to men and women in marriage, and they are all predicated on the idea that the man leads and his wife follows; that he will provide for (work outside the house and earn money) himself and his wife, and later on, his family; and that a woman will obey her husband, bear his children and raise them to be obedient and devout. Marriage, as rooted in religion, is based on the inherent assumption that a man is greater than a woman, that a woman must be subservient to her husband in all matters, everywhere, and that a man is the natural head of the family. All major religions state, explicitly or implicitly, that a wife has no agency over her own body, and must be available to her husband whenever he wants to have sex with her. In most countries, women actually change their names and adopt their husband's, and the children they bear carry his name, too. In most families, women are told to be humble, obedient and accommodating if they want to be good wives, and that their lives will effectively end the minute their marriages do. These are the assumptions that a marriage is based upon, these are the factors that make a marriage *work*.

None of this is true anymore, and the schism would be enough to drive any woman crazy. I grew up with everyone around me, including my parents, saying I was equal to boys and men, and shouldn't let anyone tell me otherwise. Just personally, I know I'm not going to spend my days beautifying myself and my home, warming damp hand towels in the microwave so my husband can wipe his face luxuriously when he gets home (I swear I read this in an issue of *Good Housekeeping* a child, and you must believe me, because I could hardly make such a thing up). I'm never going to think that my husband is my saviour, my god or even my only option, and if you live your life and have even just a *few* experiences, you simply won't be able to see him as the larger-than-life figure that marriage necessitates you must.

Today, women like me don't really need to put up with their husbands' excesses and shortcomings, with their outbursts and outpourings, inattention or infidelity. Today, more women than at any other point in modern history, have the emotional, social and financial means to at least theoretically leave their husbands if they aren't treating them right, and I think this is a big blow to the institution of marriage itself. I believe that the concept of marriage is unofficially based on women necessarily putting up with men's shit, and I actually feel rather gleeful at the institution failing and falling in the face of women refusing to do this.

I've also had the benefit of seeing many heterosexual, but still varied, kinds of marriage around me while growing up. Of these, the women who didn't subscribe vaguely to the ideals I just mentioned, or alternatively, had not grown up with the expectation of not having jobs and spending their lives serving their husbands to the best of their abilities, appear, overwhelmingly, rather unhappy with their romantic lives. They seem to be in their marriages simply because they are, because they had committed to being in them at some time in the past, and it was just too much trouble not to be in them anymore.

Some of my friends, my age-mates and classmates, have actually gone ahead and got married already. The first few years seem really nice, but soon enough, the Instagram Stories and Facebook posts professing their love, devotion and wonderment (and also making subtle-but-not-subtle references to their husbands' manliness or sexiness) begin to dwindle. By their third anniversaries, they post long, thoughtful updates talking about making it through life's ups and downs; about how relationships take hard work but their partners do ultimately make it worth it;

and also appreciating their own parents and natal homes. I have a lot of uncharitable thoughts about what they'll be posting and updating five and ten years hence, but I suppose it isn't fair to just nix their marriages out of hand.

Once I realised that I wanted to stay single by choice for life, I also discovered that in many ways, I am grossly ill-equipped to do so. Most inputs in my life that led up to here came with the expectation of impending marriage.

So I suddenly looked around and felt an alarming lack of female leadership, of someone to turn to for advice on how to lead a fruitful and peaceful life while single. Now, I'm happy to say, I have some role models and founts of wisdom I feel I can turn to, thanks to the work they do and the writing they put out into the world. But they're not exactly personal friends and I can hardly ring them up and ask them for advice on how to be happy, or how to deal with the particular minutiae my life will throw at me.

And so, five years ago, I set myself on a mission, partially inspired by academic Sara Ahmed's wonderful book, *Living a Feminist Life*. In it, Sara talks about equipping your 'feminist toolkit', a set of skills, understanding and beliefs that you might need as your 'tools' to help you lead a better, happier feminist life. Similarly, I embarked on a mission to adapt for myself a feminist toolkit for the single woman: the skills, knowledge and beliefs I would need in order to live a happily single life. Here's what I've been trying to equip myself with.

1. The ability to sort out my own emotions: Over time, I learnt the hard way that my extreme emotions, my day to day thoughts and feelings, my insecurities and traumas are mine to deal with. Expecting or needing someone to share this load is unfair to

them, but more importantly, it's also quite unrealistic. I can barely understand the hot mess that I am myself, and I know now that nobody else will have the time, patience, or even the ability to take that load on. So while working on not expecting another person to shoulder the burden of my admittedly wild emotions, I've also been working out exactly how to do it by myself. I've been paying attention to my moods and how they play out; my triggers and how I feel at different times of the month; I'm learning (very slowly and with great difficulty) how to meditate and calm my own mind; I turn to writing what I'm feeling exactly the way I would explain it to a partner, so that I've made a story with a finite beginning and an end out of it, as opposed to dealing with a huge amorphous cloud of negativity…many different things, but the point is, I'm trying to deal with my feelings on my own. Now if someone were to come along who could magically deal with my mess, that's excellent, but if they don't, I will still be just fine on my own.

2. Friends: I think as we get older, we stop making friends as easily, possibly because we don't meet as many new people as we did in school and college, and workplaces can be oddly competitive. As I grow older, and prepare myself to continue growing older while staying single, I realise how important it is to maintain the friendships I have, and to really pay attention to the new ones I make. This includes taking calls when I don't want to, or having tough conversations about personality traits or habits that bother me, and making up after fighting instead of just breaking off. Relationships take work, but as adults, friendships do too, and I'm learning every day the value of putting that work in.

3. Financial skills: In my teenage imagination of my adult, married life, my husband and I fell fairly comfortably into

accepted (but modern!) gender roles. I would make money at my cool, soul-satisfying job, but in those daydreams, I was also somehow cooking with a photogenic baby at my hip, while dude paid bills, invested in mutual funds, paid both our taxes, haggled with car and insurance salesmen and paid for more than half our beautiful house. This is not really how it *should* be in a marriage, and is certainly not how my own life will be. I'm learning to get over my manufactured distaste for discussing or handling money; to demand raises at work like my life depends on it (because it does); and to learn about things like stocks, bonds, investments and mutual funds. I can only hope that, some day, I will get over my middle-class-cum-wannabe-interior-designer desire to own my own house, but if I don't, hopefully I will have the money to buy that house myself.

4. Thick skin AKA confidence AKA walls to buttress self from this cold, cruel world: society or the world as we know it is sort of made and designed for couples. I hear that it makes paying taxes and owning a home easier, and it makes having children *much* more acceptable. Being single opens you up to cruel assumptions and questions—plenty of people will misunderstand you or ask you questions you don't feel like answering. Your life will be considered less on-track purely because you haven't decided to spend it all with one person, and the media and cultural objects will tell you that you're missing something, or still searching for it, so often that sometimes you'll begin to believe it yourself. Combatting this requires you to have a really thick skin, and as convinced as I am in my views on marriage, I am already beginning to feel the sting that comes with the assumptions people make about me, or from the pointed comments my aunts like to pass about my younger cousins being married already. I know that it is only

going to get much worse with time, and I'm working very hard on developing an armour against it. For now my technique, when confronted with such stimuli, is to go deep into myself and repeat, like a mantra if you will, the good things I have going for me and will have in the future, as a result of being single and living my life exactly the way I have chosen to live it right now.

5. Self-love. And if not, auto-commitment: I try to build myself up as deliberately as I can, because we live in a world that knocks women down, and single women additionally so. So I don't think it's a narcissistic project to embark upon negating that influence myself, and it is actually a very satisfying and eye-opening exercise to practise. That being said, self-love, as in true love, is hard to find, and there are days when it is simply impossible for me to be wildly in love with myself. This is why I've found it more useful to commit to myself instead: to commit to supporting myself, doing good and wholesome things for myself; to commit to being kind to myself, and forgiving, too. I've found that most marriages gain more from commitment rather than some sort of constantly passionate love, and I think this holds true for my relationship with myself as well.

I can't wait to re-read this essay every decade from now, and chuckle at my own certainty and naïveté. I wonder which parts of this will stand the test of time, and what I will feel about all those that did not.

Contributors

VINEETA BAL is a trained medical doctor and moved to research in immunology while pursuing her MD. She has spent a large part of her professional life working as a scientist at the National Institute of Immunology, New Delhi, chasing PhD students to do exciting and challenging experimental work and publishing it in professional journals. Every city she lived in—Pune, Mumbai, London and Delhi—has had its own influence on her thinking and personal growth. She has been associated with the feminist movement for more than thirty years, apart from being a foot soldier of other social movements at different times in her life. One of her concerns is equality and justice at work for women scientists. Aside from publishing professional work, she has also written on social issues in English and Marathi. She now lives in Pune.

BAMA, the most celebrated contemporary Dalit woman writer, was born in 1957, at Puthupatty in Tamil Nadu. Fighting against impossible odds she went through school and college and trained as a teacher, and as such, tries to impart values aimed at building self-esteem and social consciousness. Besides *Karukku*, her debut novel in 1992, she has authored *Sangathi, Kisumbukkaran, Vanmam, Oru Thathavum Erumayum, Kondattam, Manushi* and *Thavittu Kuruvi* in Tamil. The English translation of *Karukku* won the Crossword Book Award in 2000. In her novels as well as in her many articles, she focuses on themes related to caste domination and social discrimination. Her works have been translated into several languages, including English, French, Telugu, Kannada, Malayalam and Gujarati. Bama, who spent a few years in a convent as a nun, has been at the forefront of Dalit literary activism and has given Dalit aesthetics a visibility it had previously lacked.

ASMITA BASU happened upon singledom accidentally and has grown to enjoy it over the years. When not reading golden-age detective novels or discussing cabbages and kings with friends, she works as Programmes Director at Amnesty India. Basu has worked for two decades on women's rights and human rights, and has contributed to drafting laws on violence against women in India, Bangladesh, Lao PDR and Myanmar. Over time, she has also honed her talent at binge-watching movies (both pulp and arthouse), following the news as a spectator sport and travelling to exotic countries on a shoe-string budget.

ADITI BISHNOI is an editor at Women Unlimited. She has previously worked at Women's Feature Service, a not-for-profit women-centric feature syndicate, as an editor and writer focusing on issues of gender, development, child rights and climate change. Before that she covered lifestyle trends, art, music and food for various magazines published by Media Transasia (now Burda Media India). She is the co-editor of *Across the Crossfire: Women and Conflict in India* and *Women's Employment: Work in Progress.* Books, sneakers, an antiquated ipod and coffee... are a few of her favourite things!

SHERNA GANDHY has worked for various publications in Mumbai, including *Eve's Weekly, The Illustrated Weekly of India* and the *Sunday Observer*, in addition to the *Pune Times* and *Times of India*'s Pune edition. She is now a freelance copy editor.

SHARANYA GOPINATHAN is a feminist writer and journalist who divides her time and attention between Bangalore and rural Kerala, and generally tries to go for jollies.

FRENY MANECKSHA is an accidental journalist who was inducted into *The Daily* in 1981 to report on women's issues despite having no experience or a degree in journalism and little gender perspective! She worked, thereafter, in various newspapers for more than two decades as a copy desk editor. She left mainstream journalism in 2005 and decided to try her hand at reporting and writing. She is the author of *Behold I Shine: Narratives of Kashmir's Women and Children*.

AHELI MOITRA is a special reporter and editorial contributor at *The Morung Express*, a newspaper in Dimapur, Nagaland. Her work entails weaving together narratives and voices of the Naga people. Earlier, she worked as a human rights researcher to understand impunity in the Indian Union and is trained in Kingian Nonviolence Conflict Reconciliation. Moitra received the 2017 Laadli Media Award for Gender Sensitivity in Reporting (Eastern Region). She has previously lived in Delhi, Muscat, Mumbai, Nottingham, London and Kathmandu.

SUJATA PATEL is National Fellow at the Indian Institute of Advanced Studies, Shimla. Earlier, she taught sociology at the Universities of Hyderabad and Pune and SNDT Women's University. An historical sensibility and a combination of four perspectives—Marxism, feminism, spatial studies and post structuralism—influences her work, which covers diverse areas, such as modernity and social theory, history of sociology/social sciences, urbanisation and city-formation, social movements and gender construction. She has written more than 60 peer reviewed papers/book chapters and is the Series Editor of *Oxford*

India Studies in Contemporary Society and *Cities and the Urban Imperative*. She is the author of *The Making of Industrial Relations*; editor of *The ISA Handbook of Diverse Sociological Traditions* and *Doing Sociology in India, Genealogies, Locations and Practices*; and has co-edited *Bombay: Metaphor of Modern India* and *Thinking Social Science in India*, among others.

RHEA SARAN is Editor-in-Chief, *Condé Nast Traveller-Middle East*. A multi-media journalist for 15 years, Saran launched Condé Nast's first print title in the Gulf region in 2013. Under her stewardship, it has become a leader in the region's luxury travel and lifestyle space. As the host of an annual luxury travel conference and a guest speaker on industry trends, she is often invited to present to and advise tourism boards and key decision-makers. Previously, she spent around six years at *GQ India*, and worked at various publications in New York, including the American edition of *Condé Nast Traveller*. She is the author of *Girl Plus One*, a novel.

KALPANA SHARMA is an independent journalist and author based in Mumbai. In over four decades as a journalist, she has worked with *Himmat Weekly, The Indian Express, Times of India* and *The Hindu*, and was Consulting Editor with *Economic & Political Weekly* and Readers' Editor with *Scroll.in*. She is the author of *Rediscovering Dharavi: Stories from Asia's Largest Slum* and has edited *Missing: Half the Story: Journalism as if Gender Matters*. She has also co-edited *Whose News? The Media* and *Women's Issues and Terror Counter-Terror: Women Speak Out*.

LAILA TYABJI is designer, writer, crafts activist and Chairperson & Founder Member of Dastkar, an NGO that works with crafts and craftspersons across India. She has studied art in Baroda, Gujarat, and in Japan, and has worked as a freelance designer in textiles, graphics, interiors, and the theatre. A six-month assignment in Kutch, Gujarat, in 1976 was the start of her engagement with artisans, which includes chikankari embroiderers in Lucknow; Lambani tribals in Karnataka; and ari, sozni, mirror-work, kantha and other textile craftspeople in Kashmir, Rajasthan, Bihar, Odisha and Bengal. She was awarded the Padma Shri in 2012. In her free time, she reads, embroiders, cooks, travels and listens to music.

SHARDA UGRA has been a totally committed and utterly addicted sports journalist for thirty years, starting her career with the Mumbai tabloid, *Mid-Day* in the same month that Sachin Tendulkar made his Test cricket debut for India. She has worked for *The Hindu*'s Mumbai bureau and *India Today* before moving to the Internet with *Espncricinfo/ESPN India*. She has written on sports, Indian sports and the issues faced by them for popular and academic publications in several countries. She enjoys chatting with athletes of all disciplines and ages, and has worked with New Zealand cricket captain and India coach, John Wright and Indian cricketer, Yuvraj Singh on their memoirs. She has felt at home in all three cities she has lived in—Mumbai, Delhi and Bangalore—and whenever asked where she originally comes from, believes the most accurate answer is: here only.